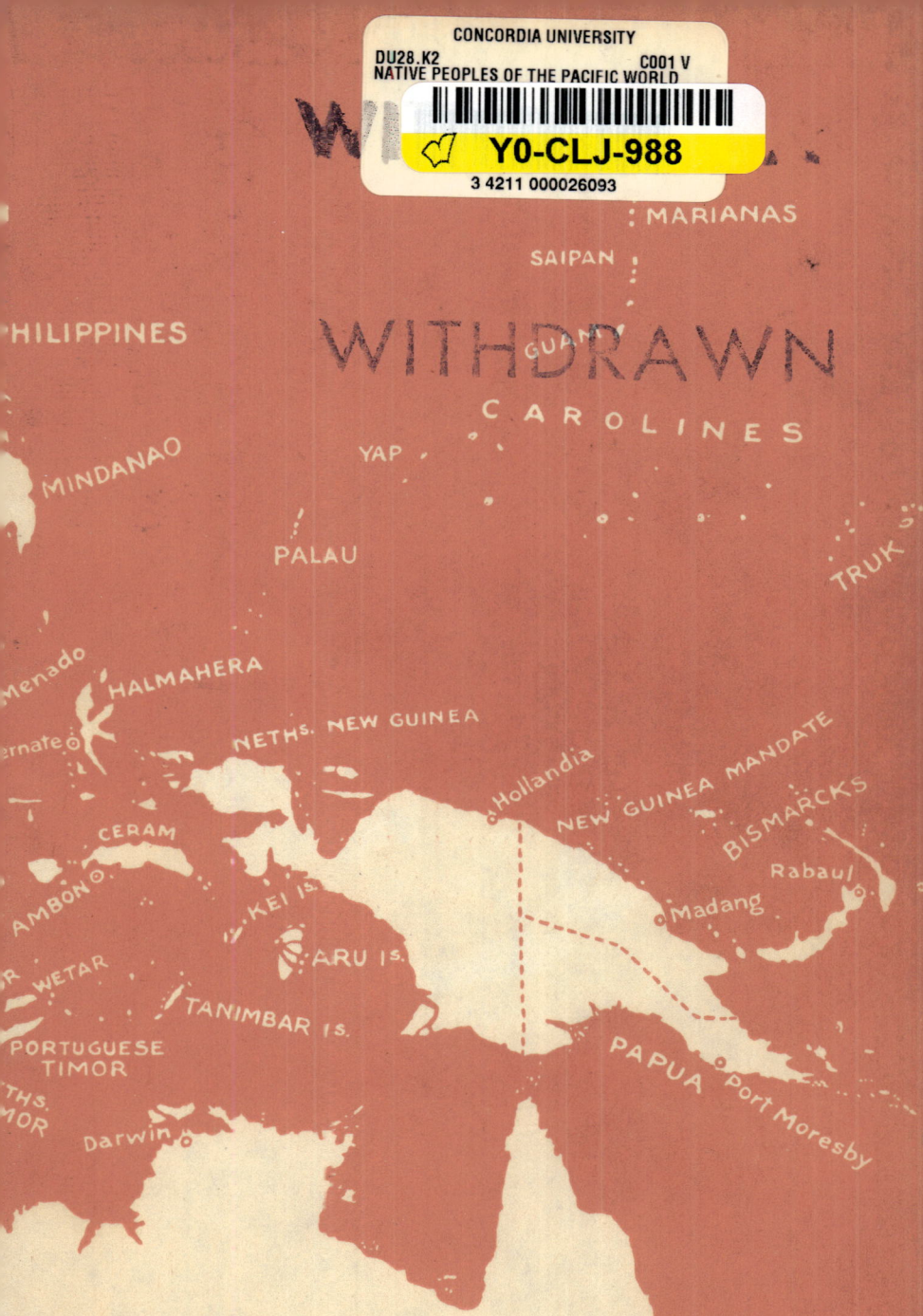

NATIVE PEOPLES
OF THE
PACIFIC WORLD

THE PACIFIC WORLD SERIES

Under the Auspices of
The American Committee for International Wild Life Protection

PUBLICATION COMMITTEE:

Fairfield Osborn, *Chairman*   Robert Cushman Murphy
Harold E. Anthony   Edward M. Weyer, Jr.
William Beebe   Childs Frick (*ex officio*)

MAMMALS of the PACIFIC WORLD
        by T. D. CARTER, J. E. HILL and G. H. H. TATE

INSECTS of the PACIFIC WORLD   by C. H. CURRAN

NATIVE PEOPLES of the PACIFIC WORLD
        by FELIX M. KEESING

REPTILES of the PACIFIC WORLD
        by ARTHUR LOVERIDGE

PLANT LIFE of the PACIFIC WORLD   by E. D. MERRILL

FISHES and SHELLS of the PACIFIC WORLD
        by JOHN T. NICHOLS and PAUL BARTSCH

THE PACIFIC WORLD
    edited by FAIRFIELD OSBORN (W. W. Norton and Co., Inc.)

NATIVE PEOPLES
OF THE
PACIFIC WORLD

Felix M. Keesing

PROFESSOR OF ANTHROPOLOGY,
STANFORD UNIVERSITY

―――――1945―――――
THE MACMILLAN COMPANY – NEW YORK

Copyright, 1945, by
FELIX M. KEESING.

All rights reserved—no part of this book may be reproduced in any form without permission in writing from the publisher, except by a reviewer who wishes to quote brief passages in connection with a review written for inclusion in magazine or newspaper.

Second Printing

A paper bound edition of this book for limited distribution was published by *The Infantry Journal*.

PRINTED IN THE UNITED STATES OF AMERICA

Foreword

THIS BOOK is one of a series describing the natural history and peoples of the Pacific Ocean and of its innumerable islands, large and small. The basin of this great ocean extends approximately halfway around the earth. Some of the islands, including most of the larger ones, were in earlier times actually a part of their neighboring continents. In other cases the islands arose by powerful geologic upthrusts, including volcanic eruptions, from the very bed of the ocean itself. Because of these different origins, the living things found upon the islands are of infinite variety and interest

The Pacific World Series has been sponsored, nurtured and created by men representing nine great American educational and scientific institutions. The original impulse or idea for the preparation of the series came from the American Committee for International Wild Life Protection. This committee not only hoped but believed that a fuller understanding of the wonder and beauty of natural things by men in the armed services in the present great war, as well as by their families and friends at home, would create a desire to protect and conserve the natural life of the islands which, if once destroyed, can never be replaced. At the same time a presentation of the natural history of the Pacific islands would not be complete without a description of the peoples who inhabit the islands. Consequently it is eminently fitting that this book should be included in this series.

Anthropology, like other sciences, can be dull and uninteresting or exciting and stimulating, depending on how it is presented. Occasionally a scientist-author appears who is able to illuminate his subject with such a light that it becomes alive. In its simplest terms, the purpose of anthropology is to bring about an understanding of peoples of all times and places. In this instance, the author has most competently and engagingly fulfilled this purpose in that his book establishes a feeling of intimacy with the numerous and diverse native peoples of the Pacific. His approach is typified by the opening chapter, entitled "Getting Acquainted." Throughout the book one is carried along through a sequence of similar approaches so that at the end one can almost say, "I really feel as if I knew those people."

It is, in a way, no wonder that Professor Keesing has been able to make such a successful presentation. Members of his family were among the early settlers in the South Pacific, including a great-grandfather who was one of the first missionaries in Fiji. The author himself first saw the light of day in one of the native states of Perak in Malaya, where his father was a surveyor in the tin areas. Professor Keesing was brought up in New Zealand, received his first university training there, followed by studies at American universities and the London School of Economics and Political Science. He got what he calls his "first slant" on anthropology through boyhood contacts with and studies of the Maoris in New Zealand. In the years since 1921 he has travelled the South Seas, the Orient, European museums and colonial centers in furtherance of his knowledge. For a period of eight years commencing with 1934, he used Hawaii as the main operating base for his studies, and during that period was attached to the University of Hawaii as Professor of Anthropology. After Pearl Harbor he was called to work in one of the war agencies in Washington, and participated in the training of naval officers for military government in the Pacific areas at Columbia University. He is at present Professor of Anthropology at Stanford University in California, where he has also taken part in the preparation of military personnel

FOREWORD

for duties in the Pacific. The materials of this handbook were developed in the practical setting of these training programs.

As this book is published, there is a far-flung battleline over the vast areas of ocean beyond our western shore. When the battles are over destiny will still be calling the American people to the area of the far Pacific. Our soldiers and sailors who are there today will be succeeded by untold numbers of American people busying themselves in the ways of peace. This book should prove a major contribution to the understanding between peoples, which is the basis of our hopes for the future of civilization.

FAIRFIELD OSBORN
President, New York Zoological Society

Introduction

THIS IS ONE of a series of handbooks on the plant and animal life and the native peoples of "the Pacific world." Written primarily for the use of the armed forces in the Pacific war theaters, these handbooks are equally fitted to the needs of government officials and other civilians going into the region. They are also of general interest to all persons wanting to know about this fascinating and vitally important part of the earth, and the role it is playing in contemporary affairs.

The series had its origin in the desire of the American Committee for International Wild Life Protection, to supply the troops with materials which would foster appreciation and conservation of the plant and animal life in the Pacific islands, and understanding of their local peoples. A committee of interested scientists, including representatives of a number of additional institutions, brought the project to completion. The scope was also broadened to make the materials of wider and more permanent usefulness.

This handbook deals with the peoples "native" to the tropical Pacific: the Netherlands Indies, the Philippines, Formosa, and the South Seas. It does not attempt to cover the complex problems of understanding the Japanese people, the Formosan Chinese, the Ainu, the Aleuts, or other groups resident in the northwest and north Pacific island zones. To do so would be impossible within the scope of one volume.

The brown-and-dark skinned peoples here discussed number about one hundred million persons. Their island homes, scattered almost one-half of the way around the globe, have been held by the great powers in a colonial status, and in an age of air transport and modern military operations are vital to Pacific strategy and security. The peoples themselves are among the most interesting of human groups, ranging today from thoroughly Westernized persons such as an educated Filipino, Javanese, or Maori to forest pigmies and roving "sea gypsies."

The lives of most of these islanders have been profoundly affected by the war. In some ways, indeed, contact with American troops and with the new goods and ideas they bring has jolted them out of their former round much more than did the Japanese occupying forces. Helping such peoples to adjust to the modern world, and to meet their problems of welfare, provides one of the greatest challenges to the spirit of democracy and humanity today.

FELIX M. KEESING
Professor of Anthropology
Stanford University

Contents

	Foreword	v
	Introduction	ix
1	Getting Acquainted	1
2	The Island Peoples	8
3	Language	30
4	Government	39
5	Livelihood	54
6	Home Conditions	88
7	Social Customs	103
8	Religion	121
9	Closing Word	132
	Appendix A: Basic Information	134
	Appendix B: A Brief Chronology	138
	Index	141

Illustrations

PLATE		PAGE

1. Most Pacific islanders are fisherfolk and seafarers. *facing* 16
2. *Upper*—Native troops have fought for the United Nations. *Lower*—Solomon Islanders aid United States marines in setting up communication lines on Guadalcanal. *facing* 17
3. *Upper*—Members of the Philippine Women's Auxiliary Service parade in Manila prior to the Japanese occupation. *Lower*—Javanese soldier gives first aid to a Dutch officer during the reoccupation of Hollandia. *between* 24–25
4. *Upper*—The Polynesians are becoming well adjusted to modern civilization. *Lower left*—Since the days of Captain Cook, Polynesian physical characteristics have aroused admiration. *Lower right*—A Micronesian of the "Kanaka" type. *between* 24–25
5. *Upper left*—New Guinea natives of the Papuan type. *Upper right*—The Chamorro type of Guam. *Lower*—Fijian girls—examples of the so-called "Melanesian" racial type. *between* 24–25
6. *Upper left*—A Negrito boy. *Upper right*—A soldier from Timor Island serving in the Dutch Army. *Lower left*—The Balinese are famed for their beauty and grace. *Lower right*—This chief of a north Sumatra district is of the "Malayan" type. *between* 24–25
7. *Upper*—The Borobudhur—gigantic and beautiful Buddhist shrine in central Java. *Lower*—The social system and the arts today keep alive much of the old "Indo-Malayan" civilization. *facing* 32
8. *Upper*—Friendliness is a universal language, as marines found in the Solomons. *Lower*—Young New Caledonians show how fish are shot with bow and arrows. *facing* 33

ILLUSTRATIONS

PLATE   PAGE

9. *Pasar* Malay developed as a language of the market place. The "pasar" at Pajacombo in west Sumatra.   *facing* 48

10. These Solomon Island children take the chance to do a little business.   *facing* 49

11. *Upper*—A Fijian village. *Lower left*—In the early days of white contact in the South Seas, native kings arose modelled on European monarchs. *Lower right*—The Sultan of Jogjakarta, Java, in official costume, accompanied by his Dutch "elder brother," the Governor of the State.   *between* 56–57

12. *Upper*—A detachment of the Samoan Marine Battalion in American Samoa is inspected by Lieutenant General A. A. Vandergrift. *Lower left*—The Royal Armed Papuan Constabulary has been the backbone of law and order in that territory for more than half a century. *Lower right*—Islanders have been trained to take important responsibilities.   *between* 56–57

13. *Upper*—Terraced rice fields reach their greatest development among the mountain peoples of the northern Philippines. *Lower*—Water-buffaloes are used to prepare the rice fields in western Malaysia.   *between* 56–57

14. *Upper*—Fishing craft of various types at Grissee in east Java. *Lower left*—Polynesian fishermen carry their outrigger canoe up the beach. *Lower right*—Making "shell money" in the Solomons.   *between* 56–57

15. *Upper*—"Stone money" of Yap Island in the Carolines is a mark of wealth. *Lower*—The early morning market in Papeete, capital of French Oceania, is thronged with Tahitian shoppers buying seafoods of many kinds, and other native edibles.   *facing* 64

16. *Upper*—Lei sellers in Honolulu. *Lower left*—How islanders shred the flesh of a coconut to make coconut cream or pudding. *Lower right*—A Samoan youth deftly plaits a basket from a coconut palm leaf split down the middle, to carry coconuts which he has husked.   *facing* 65

ILLUSTRATIONS

PLATE PAGE

17. *Upper*—Outside a Manila church, vendors sell candles, religious books, and other sacred objects. *Lower*—Javanese women add to the family income by working in textile mills and in other industries. *facing* 80

18. *Upper*—The underground oven. *Lower*—The South Seas has its cowboys. *facing* 81

19. *Upper*—A city such as Manila shows the old and the new. *Lower*—A town in Minangkabau, Sumatra. *between* 88–89

20. *Upper*—This Malaita coastal village in the Solomons is built on an artificial island, for defense in former times against hostile inland peoples. *Lower left*—A Javanese in traditional dress. *Lower right*—A tree house in a remote part of the Philippines. *between* 88–89

21. The modest "Mother Hubbard" dress brought by missionaries to women of the South Seas has been transformed by Hawaiians into a colorful *holoku*, gown with a train. *between* 88–89

22. *Upper*—Rural transportation in the Philippines. *Lower*—A bridge on a New Guinea trail. *between* 88–89

23. *Upper*—This Karo-Batak house in Sumatra is the home of sixteen families. *Lower left*—Spirited *haka* dances of the Polynesian Maoris in New Zealand are marked by stamping feet, protruding tongues, and glaring eyes. *Lower right*—Interior of a men's house or sacred community building in the Detal region of south Papua. *facing* 96

24. *Upper*—In Samoa, the village *taupo* or ceremonial hostess, with traditional headdress and valuable mat skirt, dances with her attendants. *Lower*—In Tonga only persons of chiefly rank were allowed to play the billiard-like game called *lafo*. *facing* 97

25. *Upper*—A Melanesian "sing-sing." *Lower*—The Hawaiian *hula*; one of the varied dance styles of the Polynesian peoples, though now strongly influenced by Broadway and Hollywood. *facing* 112

ILLUSTRATIONS

PLATE   PAGE

26. *Upper left*—The famous Balinese dance expert Mario teaching his art to a pupil. *Upper right*—Movies are having a profound effect on the minds of the islanders. *Lower*—The Javanese puppet plays (*wayang*) are for the masses a source not only of entertainment but also of moral teaching.   *facing* 113

27. The traveller may come across old stone ruins in the forest or along the shore.   *between* 120–121

28. *Upper*—A group of Balinese native men during a religious ceremony on the shores of the island of Bali. *Lower*—Ritual dance connected with cultivation of *taro*; Bellona Island in the Solomons.   *between* 120–121

29. *Upper*—Mohammedan mosque at Medan, Sumatra. *Lower*—Men's house and its stone platform among the Bontok mountain people in the northern Philippines.   *between* 120–121

30. *Upper*—Christian Indonesians attending church at Ende, on the island of Flores. *Lower*—Dedication of a chapel built by the natives of Guadalcanal and presented as a memorial for the Americans who died in expelling the Japanese from their homeland.   *between* 120–121

31. Modern pageantry in the islands is still infused with the spirit of old traditions.   *facing* 128

32. The island peoples may be expected in the future to take their full share in the affairs of their homelands.   *facing* 129

FIG. 1. The Pacific island groups   8
FIG. 2. Peoples of the islands.   14
FIG. 3. The island chains.   22

1. Getting Acquainted

THIS HANDBOOK is designed primarily to help a visiting soldier or civilian to understand and make friends with the island peoples of the Pacific area. It cannot, of course, answer all his questions. The islanders differ amazingly from place to place in their customs, speech, religion, and other characteristics, and it would take volumes to describe them. This book does, however, give some of the basic facts about the peoples whom the visitor may meet, and their problems of present and future. It also suggests how to go about getting to know them: how to win their confidence and cooperation, and to avoid giving offense by breaking their taboos.

Getting along well with the local peoples in such an area is obviously a vital part of military operations, just as it is essential for any civilian who expects to travel or carry on work there. In this region, with its reef-strewn seas, tropical forests, mountains and swamps, it can make a great difference if the islanders familiar with local conditions lend their active support. Friendly natives have given United Nations forces essential aid as guides, carriers, stretcher-bearers, and construction workers. They have saved the lives of many fliers forced down on inhospitable coasts, and some have fought bravely against the Japanese. Whatever food these people are able to supply to the soldier or civilian traveler helps to relieve the burden of transport and to meet emergency needs.

For all the skill a Westerner has in machine-age technology he finds himself incredibly stupid in these island places. Yet here the local native, who might appear so lost and awkward in a skyscraper or subway, is thoroughly at home. Through practical experience won by his ancestors over the centuries he knows intimately the characteristics of the weather, the terrain, plants, and animals, and all other features of the locality. He can tell what timber will stand up best to salt water if a pier is to be built, how to ride a wave over a reef, which plants to eat if caught without food. The white man going into such an area can learn from him with the utmost profit.

Anyone who has to direct in some way the activities of natives will find it absolutely necessary to understand their habits and viewpoint. An unintentional mistake as regards their taboos, for instance, may mean that carriers will desert or a labor gang vanish. A good administrator among such peoples always has to work within the framework of the local culture, just as a politician does in his home constituency—and he has to be equally sensitive to public opinion and to the ideas the people have as to what is fair and square.

Getting along well with peoples who are very different from oneself is no easy matter. Just as their ways of living will appear strange to the visitor, so they will think he is queer in his looks and behavior. Sometimes they will be amused, though they may be too polite to show it, and at other times they will be shocked and horrified at what he does. To reach the common ground of friendship calls for plenty of imagination and sympathy, while to penetrate beneath surface appearances so as really to understand the customs, viewpoints, and feelings of such peoples demands keen sleuthing. At the same time it is intensely interesting, as Marco Polo, Captain Cook, and numerous others have found. Endless curiosity, an unobtrusive notebook, and sensitivity to the proprieties of native life are the only tool-chest needed.

Most travelers will need to discard right at the first whatever ideas they may have acquired from novels and movies about "savages." Persons familiar with the islanders have found them neither so wild nor so romantic as is popularly supposed. True, in the remotest interior of New Guinea and a few of the largest neighboring islands there are peoples even yet outside the control of the white governments, and headhunting and cannibalism may still be practiced in these "uncontrolled areas." But in the very rare event that a stranger might have occasion to drop in on them,—it would almost certainly have to be by parachute because of the rugged and virtually insurmountable terrain,—he would still stand a good chance of making friends.

Other natives are likely to have been accustomed to the presence of white men for many years, if not for generations. In some more out-of-the-way areas they may look quite wild, carrying spears or bows, wearing a minimum of clothing, and having nose-plugs or other barbaric ornaments. Such groups are encountered particularly in the region from the Moluccas and Timor eastward through New Guinea and the Solomons to the New Hebrides. As the visitor gets to know them, however, he finds that they have really shifted as far from their warlike Stone Age ancestors as Americans have from their ancestors of George Washington's day. Around the ports and plantation areas the people look much more westernized and sophisticated.

Natives who have come under government influence not only accept the white man's insistence on peace and order, but also as a rule now thoroughly appreciate the security it gives to their lives. Most of them go in normal times to the store for cloth and other goods, pay taxes, and like to do some traveling. Many have worked for years as laborers on plantations or in mines. In some places everyone has become Christian or (in the westernmost islands) Mohammedan, though in others conservative groups cling to their older religions. In peace-time the native children would usually be getting some elementary schooling; here and there an individual is a high-school or even a college graduate. A corps of native officials, including trained clerks, district and village headmen, police, and medical orderlies, is used to carry on government business. Certainly it is not a savage world in spite of the strange mixture of primitiveness and civilization.

A visitor must be wary of self-styled experts who talk glibly about the characteristics of natives. A favorite cliché is that they are like children. This may be true in the sense that they are only taking the first steps in understanding western ways, but correspondingly white men are like children as regards their grasp of what life in the native setting means. Natives may also be described as happy-go-lucky, lazy, untrustworthy, or "dumb." The visitor should not accept these superficial judgments about native behavior. Rather, he should try to find out how the natives look at life, how their minds work, what their codes and standards demand. It will then be seen that they have very different economic philosophies from those of the West, that tricking a stranger may be an approved line of conduct, and that their wits are razor-sharp about matters in which they have been trained. If the visitor is able to find out what natives are thinking about the self-styled expert, he will be amused.

Actually, to generalize about native character or "temperament" is impossible. Some groups and individuals are habitually cheerful, approachable, and talkative, while others are morose and reserved. Some work very hard, and others take life much easier. Some are highly individualistic, while others work and think best in groups. Some may be depended on to the limit, and valuables may be left around safely; while others have a tradition of treachery, deception, and lying to people outside their local group, so that they have to be watched. Some make a great show of ceremonious politeness; others appear abrupt and uncouth. Even when a white man thinks he knows some native group well, he will often be left wondering if the people have "played him for a sucker."

The Japanese have not had a good record in their dealings

with such native peoples. For all their honeyed propaganda they have won little support in the areas which they conquered. The islanders, mostly independent and spirited people, have not taken any more kindly than an American would to the bowing and kowtowing demanded by the sons of Nippon. They have felt the hard hand of the Japanese military upon their lives, ordering them around and interfering with their goods and their women. Most if not all of them have the logic to hold the Japanese responsible even when Allied bombs have to be directed against their settlements. The Christian or Islamic peoples are likely to have about as much liking for the "heathen" Japanese as has a good church-going American of the Midwest.

Yet the fact must be faced that many of the islanders are none too fond of white men, even if at first the whites may have been regarded as overwhelmingly powerful gods. The western record in the islands has been by no means a creditable one; and though abuses have been attacked by governments in recent years, the native peoples are likely to have vivid memories of land grabbing, the labor traffic ("blackbirding"), forced labor, prohibition of cherished customs, and other happenings that generated resentment. In the more advanced areas, especially the large dependencies of the western Pacific, the desire to throw off colonial control has been stirring strongly.

The visitor will have to find out for himself what the attitudes are among any given group. They may range from extreme friendliness, so that the task of establishing good relations is quite easy, to considerable ill-feeling or possibly open hostility. The majority of the islanders, perhaps, are passive and indifferent; more than anything else they would like to be left alone, just as white men probably would under the same circumstances. The Japanese have tried to capitalize on any anti-white feeling they could find. Here and there, too, German missionaries and settlers have had some pro-Axis influence. Anyone going into a new area should therefore take account of the possibility of opposition, and if it occurs will need to uncover what is back of it. In general, however, even the white man's régime at its worst is likely to seem rosy to natives who have been under Japanese control.

In any area being retaken by United Nations forces from the enemy, the natives may adopt a wary attitude because of uncertainty as to what will happen to them. Doubtless many of them are wondering whether they are to be punished for cooperating, even if under compulsion, with the Japanese. They may also be wondering what the white man will expect of them as regards unpaid taxes, unexpired labor contracts, and other obligations. In some places, after white residents left at a few minutes' notice under the threat of Japanese attack, the natives looted their properties, and in some of the remoter districts tribal wars flared up again. Everywhere in the occupied areas the natives, shaken by Allied bombings, will be wondering whether they are the objects of the white man's anger along with the Japanese.

To re-establish contact with such peoples will call for understanding and sympathy. These will be required, too, by persons responsible for relief and rehabilitation programs in the island areas, and above all by those handling the problems of these peoples in the post-war period.

A NOTE ON TERMS

The word "native" has wide currency in English to refer to the local peoples in areas such as the Pacific islands, and for want of a better term it is used here. But it is not a good one. As the islanders become educated they get to know that it often has a derogatory meaning when used by a white man, and so it is resented. Yet no general substitute appears to be available, unless cumbersome words like "indigenous," "aboriginal," or "autochthonous" are used.

When such peoples are within earshot, however, it may be best to avoid using the term "native" if there is any likelihood of giving offense. The same applies to various other labels such as "coolie," *kanaka* (literally "man"), and in the case of persons of mixed descent "half-caste" or "half-breed." Nearly always there are local names which can be used without objection, such as Javanese, Samoan, or part-Hawaiian. It is well worth training the tongue to employ these acceptable labels, as they mean much in developing friendly attitudes.

2. The Island Peoples

ANYONE WHO TRAVELS at all widely through the Pacific islands gets a sense of the differences in physical appearance, speech, and customs which led early observers to divide their peoples into several broad types. It is usual, first, to distinguish two great groups: the Malaysian or Indonesian ("island Indian") peoples in the western Pacific, and the Oceanic or South Sea peoples of the central and eastern islands. The latter group subdivides in turn into three main types: the Melanesians or peoples of Melanesia ("black islands"), the Micronesians or

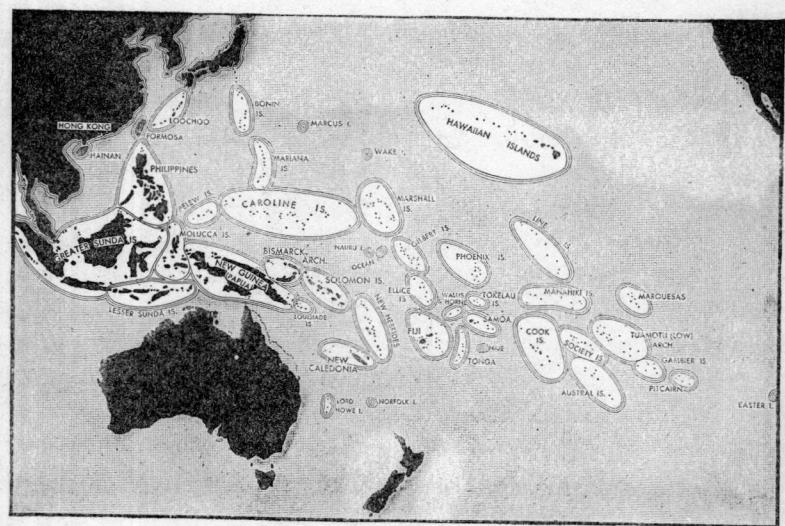

FIG. 1
The Pacific island groups.

peoples of Micronesia ("tiny islands"), and the Polynesians or peoples of Polynesia ("many islands").

The names given here are obviously scientific labels. They have as yet little if any meaning to the peoples concerned. Most of the islanders, still living within very local horizons, speak of themselves by their district, tribal, or village names.

THE POLYNESIANS

The voyager proceeding southwest from the United States comes first to the Polynesian islands, so much romanticized in stories and movies of the South Seas. They are scattered over an immense triangle of ocean, yet their combined land area, excluding New Zealand, is little more than 10,000 square miles, or about the size of the state of Maryland.

Before the whites came, the Polynesians numbered well over 1,000,000 persons. But western diseases and other death-dealing influences took such a heavy toll in the early days of contact that by the end of the last century only about 200,000 were left. At that time practically all observers prophesied that they would soon die out. Instead, as a result of health work and better adjustment to modern conditions, they are now increasing rapidly in most areas. At present they number about 350,000. The Polynesian birth-rate is high, and their villages swarm with children. A considerable amount of racial intermixture has taken place with whites and in some regions with Chinese, notably in Hawaii and New Zealand, and around the port areas of the tropical islands. But the Polynesian racial elements show no signs of being submerged.

The main Polynesian groups with their approximate numbers today are the Hawaiians (70,000 if part-Hawaiians are included), Samoans (73,000), New Zealand Maoris (100,000), Tongans (35,000), Society Islanders (25,000), Cook Islanders (17,000), Ellice Islanders (4,000), Wallis and Horne Islanders

(5,000), Tuamotuans (5,000), Austral Islanders (3,000), Marquesans (2,500), and Easter Islanders (500).

The Lau Islanders of eastern Fiji and the Rotumans on an island north of Fiji are also dominantly Polynesian. So too are small groups on several islands farther west along the outer fringe of Melanesia, such as Sikiana, Tikopia, and Rennel. These latter peoples were evidently carried there in drift canoes by the prevailing easterly winds and currents, as their histories and traditions trace them back to the main Polynesian area.

Hollywood and hula dancers have given Westerners a fairly accurate idea of the physical appearance of Polynesians. They are brown-skinned, generally tall, with hair straight to curly, and often of superb physique. By middle age many Polynesians run to bulk,—though all over the body rather than in the paunch only,—so that the average white man or woman looks puny beside them. Racially they show a combination of the physical traits associated with the white (Caucasoid), Asiatic (Mongoloid), black (Negroid), and Australian aborigine (Australoid) peoples. On some islands the white traits seem strongest, and on others the Mongoloid; the remaining two strains are minor. The racial history of the Polynesians clearly leads them back to the Malaysian region of the western Pacific, where all these physical elements are represented.

The Polynesians have been called the Vikings of the Pacific, the most daring ocean voyagers and explorers the world has ever known. Scientists reject the speculations of some people that they are the survivors of a lost and sunken continent, or that they came to the islands from America. Their traditions, their customs, their food plants and animals, and all other evidence points to the outer fringe of Malaysia, perhaps the Philippines-Celebes region, as the place from which their ancestors migrated. Probably their large ocean-going canoes struck out eastward from Malaysia early in the Christian era. En route they may have stopped for longer or shorter periods along the chain of Micronesian islands, and some may also have skirted along the northern fringe of Melanesia.

The main body of the Polynesians seems to have settled in the Society Islands, notably on Ra'iatea, though some may have gone directly to Hawaii, Samoa, and other groups. Before whites arrived, Ra'iatea was the political and spiritual hub of central Polynesia. Canoeloads of these Society Islands people later ranged out to occupy the islands from Hawaii in the north to New Zealand in the south and the Tuamotus and other islands in the east. Polynesian traditions suggest that some of their canoes sailed even into Antarctic waters, and others may have reached the shores of America. At least, by the time that white "discoverers" arrived, they had settled every habitable island in the vast spaces of the eastern Pacific, and had left their religious shrines and other traces of their passage on almost every uninhabitable speck.

Needless to say, the Polynesians were expert navigators. They knew then as they know today the lore of seasonal and weather changes, the direction of winds, waves, and currents, movements of the heavenly bodies, the sky color which hangs over a distant lagoon, the flight of birds, and the movements of fish. The early whalers and other sea captains recruited them for their crews because of these skills. Today seafaring Polynesians may be found on all the oceans of the world. Allied troops fighting and living in the islands have learned a great deal from these peoples, not only about the sea but also about how to get along comfortably on islands that may look almost barren to the inexperienced eye of the outsider.

Great numbers of the Polynesians must have lost their lives in the course of so much voyaging and pioneering. Those who survived formed a hardy breed. Beneath an often easy-going exterior, and a mode of living which has had a great appeal for the white man because of its friendliness, its giving and sharing, its singing and dancing, there is a quality of toughness and a fatalistic streak which may trace back to these ordeals of the past. Few observers have questioned the mental alertness of the Polynesians. In places where they have had the incentive to move across into the white man's civilization, notably in Hawaii and New Zealand, they have shown themselves capable. A considerable number have gone to college and have become competent doctors, lawyers, and teachers. In New Zealand several Maori members of Parliament have been Cabinet Ministers. Individuals of real genius have emerged.

The ways of living of the Polynesians show an over-all similarity: in language, in fishing methods, in an aristocratic social system by which high chiefs trace their descent directly back to the gods, and so on throughout their customs. Yet each island group, and sometimes each district on an island, has developed its own differences in the detail of speech and culture. What is known about one place will therefore carry over in a general way to another place, but nothing can be counted on as being exactly the same. The shape and tie of a fishhook or canoe outrigger, the food menu, the stories about ancient heroes, and practically every other element in the life of the people has its own local twist.

Writers on Polynesia have always been tempted to use their most flattering adjectives. To the early white voyagers who had spent months at sea in their slow sailing ships, the islands appealed as a kind of paradise. The more rugged Polynesian customs such as warfare and cannibalism soon lapsed after the coming of the whites. Before the end of the nineteenth century practically all of the Polynesians had been converted to Christianity by Protestant or Catholic missions. They had become used to depending on the trading store for cloth and other goods. The children went to school and mastered at least the rudiments of the "three R's" in their own languages. Their tribes and villages came under white political control, though

THE ISLAND PEOPLES 13

usually a great amount of self-government has been left to their own chiefs and councils.

Yet along with all such changes the Polynesian peoples have held conservatively to many of their old customs and beliefs. This has been true even of groups living around the towns and ports. They are by no means convinced that the white man's ways are wholly superior to their own. Polynesians still depend to a large extent on their traditional kinds of fishing and gardening for a livelihood. Their kinship and tribal systems are still very much alive, though a little shaken as the younger people begin to succumb to the go-getting individualism of the West. They spend much time and effort on their traditional ceremonies, and feasting, dancing, and music are essentials of living. Devout Christians though they usually are, they often seem far more afraid of their local spirits and ghosts than of hell-fire. Their sex life, rooted in a very different morality from that of the white man, continues to be the despair of missionaries.

Any visitor is certain to be fascinated in observing the adjustment these peoples have made between old and new ways. He can also see how closely their lives are shaped to the unusual conditions of their island setting, and is likely to conclude that western civilization has only a limited amount to offer which is better than what they have worked out for themselves.

THE MICRONESIANS

West from Polynesia and almost wholly north of the equator are the tiny islands of Micronesia. The great majority are low coral rings (atolls) and islets, but a small number are higher volcanic islands, notably Kusaie, Ponape, the chain of the Marianas, and clusters of small islands within the lagoons of Truk and Palau. Usually the Micronesian area is thought of as having many hundreds of islands, and this would be true if all the little ribbons of land and sandbanks along the edges of the atolls were to be counted separately. But it is more realistic to picture Micronesia as containing somewhat over a hundred distinct island units, of which about eighty are inhabited. Their combined land area is only about 1,200 square miles, or one-quarter the size of the state of Connecticut.

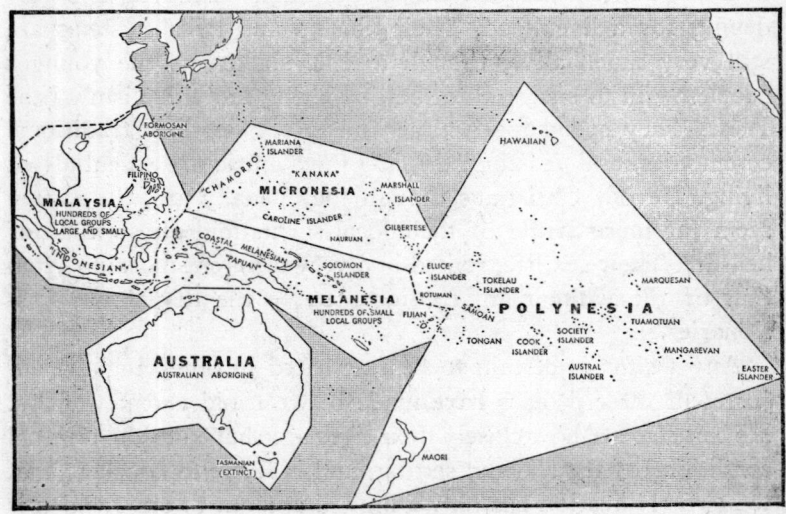

Fig. 2
Peoples of the islands.

The principal Micronesian peoples are the Gilbertese (numbering today approximately 32,000), the Ocean and Nauru Islanders (close to 2,000 each), the Marshall Islanders (10,000), various groups labeled collectively the Caroline Islanders (30,000), the Palau and Tobi Islanders (6,000), the Guamese (23,000), and the people of the Japanese Marianas (4,000). A few small islets on the northern fringe of New Guinea and the Bismarcks, such as the Northwestern Islands, have a predominantly Micronesian population. Like the Polynesians these people declined rapidly in numbers at the earlier stages of contact. Some islands, notably Yap, appear to be still showing a downward movement. But the general trend now seems to be upward, especially in Guam where the population is increasing rapidly. The total number of Micronesians today is about 110,000.

The unity of Micronesia lies perhaps more in its geography than in its inhabitants. Each cluster of islands, and sometimes an island speck off by itself, has developed along its own lines of language, of custom and even to some extent of race. In general, however, the Micronesians form a link between the Polynesians to the east and the Asiatic peoples farther west.

The eastern Micronesians such as the Gilbert and Marshall peoples are physically much like Polynesians. Farther west the Mongoloid traits increase, so that the western Micronesians are more like the Malaysian peoples of the adjacent Philippines and of the Formosan mountains. The racial pattern here has been complicated by the fact that many Filipinos settled and married among the western islanders during Spanish times, and the Spaniards themselves added a strong racial strain through intermarriage. Guam was a special center for such mingling, and the old native elements have long since been merged into a fused population of modern days. Other strains—white, American Indian, Negro, and Japanese—have touched the Micronesian here and there, and in the southern islands a darker Melanesian heritage also appears to have entered into this racial mélange.

The Micronesians of today are divided into two main groups. One, called "Chamorro," consists of western Micronesians such as the Guam people, who are for the most part racially mixed and who speak a language called Chamorro which is strongly marked by Spanish and Filipino speech. The other, known as "Kanaka," from the Polynesian word for "man," comprises people still wholly or mainly of native background and located principally in central and eastern Micronesia. The Micronesians, however, have little if any sense of common identity, even to this extent.

Like the Polynesians these islanders are seafarers, and win a large part of their livelihood from the ocean. They are particularly skilled in weaving and basketry, and the Gilbertese even used to make elaborate suits of armor out of coconut and other fibers. They also have wicked-looking weapons and tools studded with sharks' teeth. Much the same changes have taken place during modern days as in the tropical Polynesian islands. The majority of the people are now Christians, mainly Catholics in the west, where Spanish missionaries have been at work since the late sixteenth century, and Protestants in the east, where American and British missions came nearly three centuries later. There is the same conservatism, perhaps even stronger because of the checkered political history of the islands.

Most parts of Micronesia have had a succession of imperial rulers. The Gilberts and Ocean Island have been an exception. They were from the first under British control, and today their peoples have advanced to the point where each island is virtually self-governing. But the nearby Marshalls and Nauru were first German, then the former became part of the Japanese mandate and the latter a British mandate controlled from Australia. Guam shifted in 1898 from Spanish to American rule. The remaining islands of Micronesia—the Carolines, Palaus, and northern Marianas—have been held successively by Spain, Germany, and then Japan. It can hardly be wondered at that many of these islanders seem to show a very passive and negative attitude toward outsiders and their ways. In recent years Japanese immigrants and military forces have largely pushed aside the Micronesians in their mandate, and this has made them willing enough to cooperate with American forces as the Japanese have been ousted from their island homes.

PLATE 1
Most Pacific islanders are fisherfolk and seafarers.

Press Assn. and U.S. Marine

PLATE 2

Upper. Native troops have fought for the United Nations. Lord Gowrie, Governor-General of Australia, inspects a Papuan infantry unit in New Guinea.

Lower. Solomon Islanders aid U.S. marines in setting up communication lines on Guadalcanal; the native peoples are capable of handling skilled activities.

THE MELANESIANS

The Melanesians, sometimes called "Oceanic Negroids," occupy the numerous tropical islands to the north and northeast of Australia. Included are the huge island of New Guinea, more than twice the size of Japan proper, and the great archipelagoes which run eastward to New Caledonia and Fiji. On the other side of New Guinea the Melanesian racial heritage is strong in the Molucca-Timor region, but farther west it gives way progressively to the more Mongoloid strains characteristic of southeast Asia. Altogether the Melanesian islands add up to nearly 400,000 square miles, or more than one-eighth the size of the United States.

This region is one of the great empty frontiers of the earth. Though census-taking here is anything but accurate, the Melanesians appear to total about 2,000,000 persons, or an average of only about five to the square mile. Dutch New Guinea has perhaps about 500,000. Papua (the southeast part of New Guinea, with its offshore islands) 350,000, northeast New Guinea 550,000, the Bismarck area 200,000, the Solomons (including Bougainville and Buka) 150,000, the New Hebrides 40,000, New Caledonia and the Loyalties 30,000, and Fiji 110,000.

How uncertain these figures are for Melanesia becomes apparent when it is realized that a considerable part of interior New Guinea and of nearby New Britain Island has not yet been penetrated by whites or brought under government control. Most of the western Melanesian islands were little known until well along in the nineteenth century. Their reef-strewn waters and malarial coasts, and the evil repute of their warlike inhabitants, caused most voyagers to give them a wide berth. Subsequently, however, the peoples of the smaller islands and of the accessible coasts and river valleys of the large islands were pacified. Many are now Christians, and tens of thousands of the men have worked as contract laborers on the white man's plantations and in other enterprises. Around the ports and in the more developed regions such as Fiji, New Caledonia, and the Gazelle Peninsula of New Britain (the Rabaul area), they are well along in the footsteps of the Polynesians.

Some parts of Melanesia are still undergoing depopulation, notably in the Solomons and the New Hebrides. Here the visitor may see abandoned villages, or settlements in which the people are mostly old. But the Melanesians appear to be passing out of this phase of disastrous contact with white civilization, and in many places they are definitely known to be increasing. Where villages have large numbers of children and young people it is a rather sure sign that they are on the upgrade. Much less intermixture has taken place here than in Polynesia and Micronesia, though a few "half-castes" may be noted, usually around the ports.

Scholars often narrow down the term "Melanesian" to refer to one section or type of these dark peoples, distinguishing out another type to which they give the name "Papuan," from a Malay word meaning "frizzly-haired." This takes account of the fact that the islanders fall broadly into two groupings, though the exact lines between them are hard to draw. Perhaps the clearest distinction is in language, as will be shown in the next chapter, but physical differences are also fairly marked.

The Papuan type is usually of medium height, and has strongly chiseled features, sometimes with a long aquiline nose and full, heavy lips. Persons of this type appear to show a considerable strain of the same racial materials as the nearby Australian Aborigine—so-called Australoid features—combined with the dark Negroid elements uppermost in the region. As might be expected on grounds of geography, they are found most frequently in the western and southern parts of New Guinea, nearest Australia. This strain also occurs here and there in the interior of the larger islands farther to the east, and in New Caledonia at the end of the main chain.

The Melanesian type by contrast is generally somewhat taller, less heavily featured (at times even snub-nosed), with a large bush of frizzly hair. Sometimes the skin is darker than that of the Papuan and sometimes lighter. Persons of the Melanesian type are concentrated more along the coasts of the large islands, including the north and east of New Guinea, and on the small islands east to Fiji. Much the same physical characters are often found farther west in those parts of the Molucca-Timor region and of east Flores not settled by the Malayan peoples. To complicate the picture even further, the more remote inland parts of New Guinea and some of the other islands are peopled by scattered groups who are very short in stature, some of them even being down to pigmy size, hence often called Pigmy Papuans in the west and Melanesian Negritos farther east in Melanesia.

Theorists are puzzled in their attempts to unravel this racial tangle in the Melanesian islands. The temptation has been to say offhand that black peoples, some tall, some short, moved here from the African region. Farther west in the forests of the Malaya-Philippines area there are still pigmy-sized Negritos ("little Negroes") who seem undoubtedly related to the Melanesian pigmies, and such peoples were once much more widely scattered in southeast Asia than they are now. But no signs exist of tall Negroes in the area. Perhaps the safest guess, therefore, is that the peoples of Melanesia have been compounded from the undoubtedly old Australoid and Negritoid strains which were carried in by early migrants from southeast Asia, combined to some extent with taller strains added later, especially in the case of the coastal Melanesians, by way of what will be spoken of below as Indonesian or Proto-Malay type peoples.

Melanesia is a region of extreme cultural contrasts. Marked

differences in speech and custom occur not only from district to district but also frequently from community to community. In the New Guinea area, for example, the peoples living on small offshore islands and along the coasts are nearly always fisherfolk, and some are great traders, selling fish, shells, and other marine products to the inland groups. In the mountains the people are likely to be intensive gardeners, though some gain an important part of their livelihood by gathering forest products and by hunting. The river peoples may do some fishing, while groups living in the swampy deltas and fresh-water marshes may have sago as a principal food. Some Melanesian peoples are friendly and approachable; others are sullen and suspicious of strangers. Here a group is noisy and merry, while another is taciturn. The visitor will be astonished at the many variations they have worked out for, say, the shape of a house or the fashion of a geestring or pubic covering.

Taking note of so many contrasts, it is virtually impossible to give any list of characteristics that can be called typical of Melanesia. Usually the people live in independent little settlements which formerly were at war with neighbors, and still may be in the remote interior of the larger western islands. Their marriage, family, and other social customs are often so strange that it is hard for anyone not brought up in the society to understand them. Many groups have elaborate secret societies into which persons are admitted only by undergoing long and fantastic initiation ceremonies; a visitor may see some of the masks and other colorful paraphernalia of such societies. Religious ideas are likely to revolve particularly around the ghosts of the dead, who are believed to continue to influence the living so that rites of many kinds have to be performed to keep them in a happy frame of mind.

The Melanesians also differ vastly in their degree of contact with modern civilization, by way of government control, the trading store, missions, the labor barracks, and schools. In eastern Melanesia the Fijians and New Caledonians are now practically all Christians, and they are well along in their adjustment to civilization. Fijians may be seen wearing high-school blazers, and several have college degrees. In the Solomons it is an exceptional man who has not spent three years or more working away from his home village as a contract laborer, during which time he has gained a rough-and-ready knowledge of the outside world. Well over half the Solomon Islanders are Christians, and the white man's government has by now entered deeply into the fabric of native life in such an area. Much the same is true in the New Hebrides and in the more accessible parts of the New Guinea region. Before the war the frontier of western penetration and influence was being pushed back steadily year by year into the deep interior by special government patrols.

THE MALAYSIANS

Malaysia is centered upon the Great Sunda islands, that is, Sumatra, Java, Borneo, and the Celebes. On the north side it takes in the Philippines and the mountainous eastern half of Formosa, which has a so-called Aborigine population closely related to the Philippine mountain peoples. Malaysian racial characteristics also appear to form one of the important elements that have gone to the making of the Loochoo (Ryukyu) Islanders and even of the Japanese people. On the east side Malaysia merges with Melanesia in the eastern Lesser Sundas area. Westward the Malay Peninsula marches racially with Malaysia, and many peoples on the coasts and in the hills of Thailand, Burma, Indochina, and south China show strong marks of this heritage. In fact, no clear line can be drawn between the Malaysians and the so-called "yellow" or Mongoloid peoples living farther north in Asia.

Portuguese voyagers reached the Malaysian islands in 1509.

At that time there were perhaps 10,000,000 people in the area. Today there are close to 100,000,000 Malaysians. The greatest increase in numbers has been in the last half century, during which the over-all population of Malaysia has about doubled. Such increase has taken place mostly in the rich deltas and valley areas and on the flat coastal plains where rice is intensively cultivated, and in the industrially developed areas such

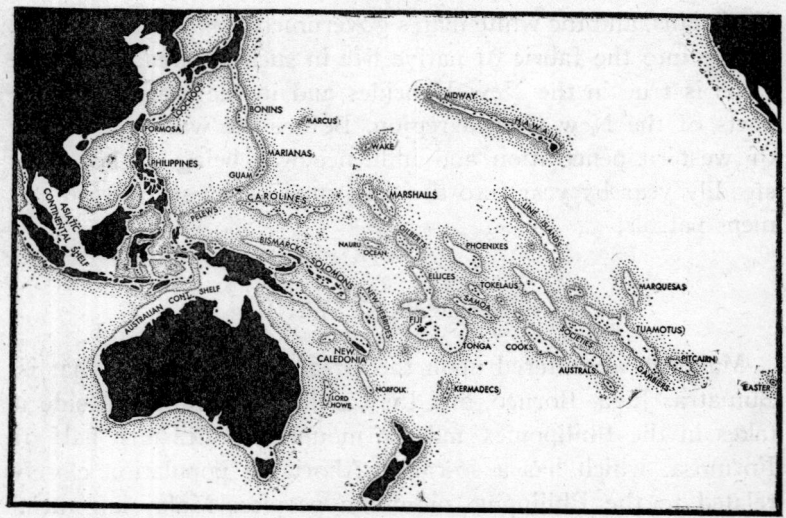

FIG. 3
The Island Chains.

as Java and the Manila region of the Philippines. By contrast, mountainous and swampy districts and the less accessible coasts are still for the most part thinly populated.

Few people realize the great size of these Malaysian islands. Borneo is 284,000 square miles in area, or almost twice as large as Japan proper, though its total population is only about 3,800,000. Sumatra, with 183,000 square miles, or one and one-half times the size of Italy, has about 9,250,000 inhabitants.

Java, with 51,000 square miles, or about the size of New York State, has the amazing total of over 50,000,000 persons, and this figure is rising by over a half million every year. The Philippines, with 114,400 square miles, have more than 17,000,000, or well over twice as many as when the United States acquired the islands. Altogether the Malaysian areas total about 800,000 square miles, or more than one-fourth the size of the United States.

Malaysia might be looked upon as a huge mixing bowl into which, through thousands of years, human groups migrating from Asia have deposited their varying quotas of racial ingredients. In turn, these have spilled over the other side of the bowl from time to time into the Oceanic areas. Here and there within the bowl, lumps of the old materials have managed to keep their identity in the cracks and eddies—that is, in the deep forests, mountains and swamps—and therefore may still be seen today. The mass of humans in the region, however, now consists of various mixtures and fusions.

First into the bowl, perhaps a half-million years ago, came the shadowy figure of the Java "ape-man," *Pithecanthropus*, known only through his fossil remains in east-central Java. Scientists regard him as a cousin rather than a direct ancestor of modern types of man, and apparently he became extinct long before the first humans proper arrived. These were tiny nomadic bands of Stone Age hunters, variously of Australoid and Negritoid types, who probably came during the last great Ice Age, which was at its maximum about 25,000 years ago. At this time much more of the earth's water was frozen at the poles and in glaciers than now, so that the sea-level may have been as much as 200 feet lower than it is today. Furthermore, the shallow continental shelfs on which most of the islands in the Malaysian and Australian areas rest may have been higher at that time, for they show signs of having subsided here and there. If such speculations are correct, these early peoples could have walked across land bridges into Java and the Philippines, and by crossing a few narrow channels on rafts or in crude canoes could also have reached New Guinea and Australia.

Later, after the land bridges had been flooded over by deepening waters, other migrants came into the islands by boat. Perhaps as early as 8,000 years ago, brown-skinned peoples who had been compounded in the adjacent mixing bowls of India and southeast Asia began to settle in Malaysia. These groups are usually called either Indonesians ("island Indians") or Proto-Malays ("proto" means "first"). They appear to have been dominantly of white (Caucasoid) racial heritage but perhaps with mixtures of Australoid and Negritoid. Peoples somewhat like them may be found in India today, especially along the eastern coastal districts.

Probably about 3,000 years ago, peoples with more Mongoloid racial traits began to arrive in Malaysia. The smooth features, straight hair, and yellow-brown skin color which they brought are characteristic of the region of Asia north of the Himalayas. In time these became the predominant elements in western Malaysia, especially in the smaller islands and in the lowlands of the large islands. The racial type which has these characters emphasized is often called Malayan or Deutero-Malay ("deutero" meaning "second").

Many different variations and combinations of these racial materials occur in different localities and from person to person in Malaysia today, products of nature's experiments in human breeding over many generations. Any Negro-like traits, and much of the general shortness of stature in the region, seem to lead back to the Negritoid heritage. The forests and swamps of Malaya and the eastern Philippines still have Negrito remnants, as noted already—shy nomads who live on wild forest plants and game. In the mountains of Malaysia, just as farther east in the Pacific, tall Indonesian strains may be encountered. The name "Alfur" is sometimes applied to peoples in the

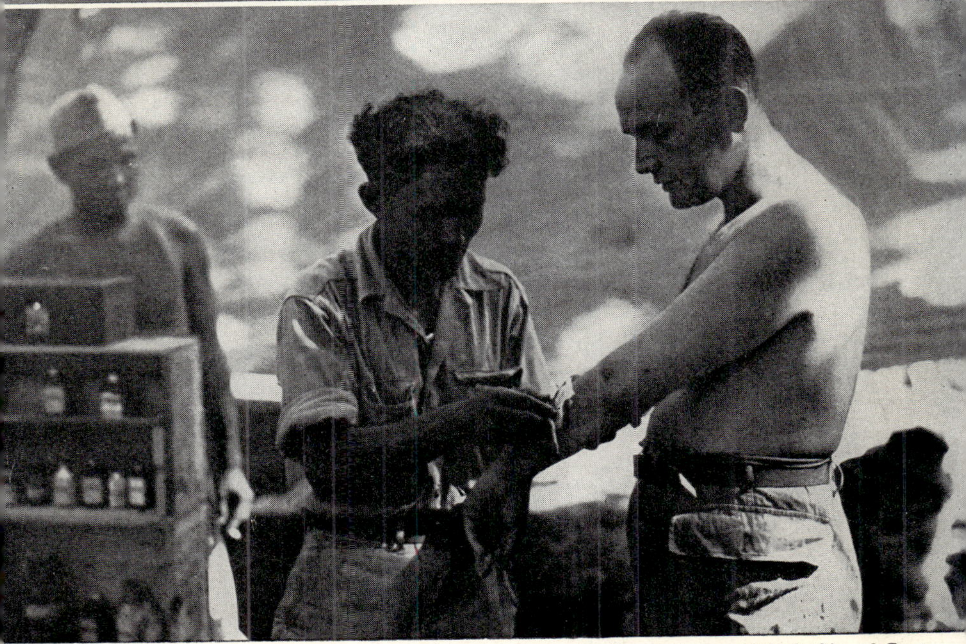

Press Assn. and U.S. Signal Corps

PLATE 3

Upper. Members of the Philippine Women's Auxiliary Service parade in Manila prior to the Japanese occupation.

Lower. Javanese soldier gives first aid to a Dutch officer during the reoccupation of Hollandia.

Pan Pacific Press and British

PLATE 4

Upper. The Polynesians are becoming well adjusted to modern civilization—a Hawaiian and his daughter.

Lower left. Since the days of Captain Cook, Polynesian physical characteristics have aroused admiration.

Lower right. A Micronesian of the "Kanaka" type. The long hair of this elderly Gilbertese indicates that he is of the old school.

Archbold Expeditions, U.S. Navy and Matson Navigation Co.

PLATE 5

Upper left. New Guinea natives of the Papuan type. These isolated people of the Balim River valley of Dutch New Guinea still use stone age axes. One man has a pig's tusk piercing his nose.

Upper right. The Chamorro type of Guam: These girls escaped through the Japanese lines when American forces stormed the island.

Lower. Fijian girls—examples of the so-called "Melanesian" racial type.

American Museum of Natural History, Netherlands Information Bureau and Claire

PLATE 6

Upper left. A Negrito boy. Pigmy size is about 4 feet 10 inches or less.
Upper right. A soldier from Timor in the Dutch army. Most Timor natives, like other peoples of the eastern Lesser Sundas and the Moluccas, are of the Negritoid-Australoid types rather than the Malayan.
Lower left. The Balinese are famed for their beauty and grace. Taller than the Javanese, they are of the Indonesian type.
Lower right. This chief in northern Sumatra is of "Malayan" type.

Celebes, Moluccas, and eastern Lesser Sundas who represent the transition between the Malayan and the Papuan types. Everywhere faces will hint at the varied elements which come together in Malaysia: Australoid, Negritoid, Indonesian, Mongoloid—plus, of course mixtures with later immigrant strains from India, Arabia, China, Europe, and America. In recent centuries considerable intermixture has taken place between the earlier peoples and these incoming groups; in the Philippines, persons recognized as of mixed ancestry are called *mestizos,* and in the Indies "Indo-Europeans," "Indo-Chinese," and other hyphenated names.

In early times the Malaysian peoples were broken up into small independent tribes, communities, or bands, with a Stone Age type of life. Many groups continued to live at this level of political development up to modern days. Shortly before the Christian era, however, the western sections of Malaysia began to come under the influence of civilization as it was developing in adjacent India. The basis was laid for a brilliant though little-known period in Malaysian history.

A busy sea-borne trade started up at this time between the Indians and Arabs on the one side of Malaysia and the Chinese on the other. Inevitably places like Sumatra, Java, and Indochina became of importance, for they commanded the vital straits through which such commerce had to pass. Indian, Arab, and Chinese merchants settled at strategic port areas, and soon local products of the Indies, notably spices and gold, were flowing into these trade channels. With the Indian and Chinese traders came monks and missionaries, first of the Brahman faith, then Buddhist. India was at this time the scene of a struggle between these two great religions, and first one and then the other appears to have been carried over by refugees who found haven in Malaysia. Princes of royal houses in southeast India appear to have come too, and by force or invitation became rulers of petty states which were consolidating around the principal trade centers. The working of metals, elements of the Sanskrit language, religious art and architecture, and many other features of Indian culture were carried into southeast Asia in these early centuries. The Greek geographer Ptolemy was able to draw a fairly good map of this area about 150 A.D., and Roman emperors used the spices of the East.

By the eleventh century, a number of powerful Indo-Malayan states had become established. In Sumatra, a colorful realm called Sri-Vishaya, with its capital near present-day Palembang, exercised imperial control over much of Malaysia. Apparently the Sumatrans built the stupendous Buddhist shrine called the Borobudhur in central Java, one of the architectural wonders of the world. On the mainland the rulers of the Khmer or Cambodian state were embellishing their capital, Angkor, with elaborate temples and other structures. So, too, were the rulers of Annam and Champa in the eastern part of Indochina, Pagan in interior Burma, and other important states. Later, most of these early realms were to be devastated, Pagan by Mongol troops of Kublai Khan, Khmer by aggressive Thai peoples who were moving down from the interior mountains to form modern Siam (Thailand), Champa by its northern neighbor Annam, and Sri-Vishaya by a nearby people whom the Sumatrans never were able to subdue—the Javanese.

The modern drama and poetry of Java keep alive a "golden age" in which its people not only destroyed the power of their Sumatran neighbors—Sri-Vishaya's capital was razed in 1377 —but also ruled over a large part of Malaysia. Chinese and Arab chroniclers tell of early Javanese states such as Kediri, from where ships traded even to Madagascar off the east coast of Africa. But the high point of Javanese history came with the development of a powerful state and empire known as Madjapahit, which was at its zenith about the end of the fourteenth century. The rulers of Madjapahit were thought of as incarnations of Brahman and Buddhist deities, and the tremendous respect of the Javanese today for their princes and other high-born persons appears to be rooted in such beliefs.

The imperial power of Madjapahit waned in the fifteenth century. Still another wave of religion was sweeping through Malaysia by this time—Mohammedanism, or as its followers call it, Islam. Moslem Arabs had been trading in the region long before, yet they made little attempt to spread the doctrines of the Arabian Prophet who had founded their faith in the early seventh century A.D. Large sections of India and parts of China had meanwhile become Mohammedan, but in Malaysia only a few groups near the northwest tip of Sumatra had been converted.

Early in the fifteenth century, the important port of Malacca on the Malay Peninsula, founded, so tradition says, by refugees from fallen Sri-Vishaya, came under Mohammedan control. A group of Islamic missionaries called *sayyids,* who claimed to be descendants of the Prophet, turned their attention to the Malaysian area. Through conquest and intermarriage they spread their faith outward from Malacca. Madjapahit's capital was taken by the Mohammedans toward the end of the fifteenth century. Some of the important families fled eastward to nearby Bali, which has remained the last stronghold of the old Brahman-Buddhist faith up to modern times.

Moslem power continued to spread through the more accessible parts of Malaysia. In the Philippines its march was finally stopped with the coming of the Christian Spaniards in the mid-sixteenth century. Malaysia under Islamic control broke up into hundreds of separate states, most of them small, ruled by sultans or rajahs who usually traced their ancestry back to Mohammed by way of the *sayyids*. More than three hundred of these states continue to be vigorous today, having been incorporated by the Dutch, British, and other imperial authorities into their colonial governments, and given a large measure of self-rule. The control of Mohammedan peoples in this way by Christian powers is naturally a very delicate matter, and official policies have been to interfere as little as possible with anything which touches upon Islamic law and custom.

In the early sixteenth century the Portuguese captured Malacca and the Moluccas ("Spice Islands"), and so took control of the rich trade of the Indies. Soon after this the Spaniards moved into the Philippines, conquering all but the Islamic southern areas. During the first part of the seventeenth century the Dutch ousted the Portuguese from all their Malaysian holdings except the eastern part of Timor. Later the British established themselves in what became known as the Straits Settlements, and the French in Indochina. From these imperial beginnings the modern colonial pattern has been woven.

At first the European powers were interested in little beyond commerce; this was the time of the fabulous East India Companies. But of necessity they had to establish political control at key points to protect their trade. They also made numerous treaties with the local native rulers in order to secure their spheres of influence. Yet in the outer parts of Malaysia—that is, away from Java, the Philippine lowlands, and a few other centers of development—it was not until the late nineteenth or early twentieth century that modern-style administration was established. This is important for the visitor to know. In these remoter areas there will be people still living who saw white troops march into their territories, and the powers of their traditional rulers or chiefs curbed. Even where the younger generation may be thoroughly appreciative of the new order of things, some of the elders may be more conservative.

Looking over Malaysia today, therefore, very great differences are seen among its peoples in their physical characteristics, their degree of civilization, their beliefs, and their ways of living generally. Broadly speaking, a traveler going from west to east through this region, or from the coast up into the interior mountains of the large islands, passes through the various levels of development represented in Malaysia's history. Back from the cosmopolitan city centers such as Batavia and Manila are the lowland towns and villages, with their busy markets and intensively cultivated fields. Along with the native peoples are found Chinese, Arabs, and Indians, mainly engaged in commerce, and here and there a white or part-white (Eurasian) person, usually an official, but in some areas connected with estates or mines. Still farther back the population thins out. Pioneer native settlers from the lowlands battle the jungle, and forest and mountain folk carry on their traditional round of life often little disturbed as yet by the profound changes which have taken place in the coastal areas. The great range from the extremely modern to the little-touched savage is sensed perhaps best in Manila, where the visitor can stand on an up-to-date boulevard and look across to Mariveles Mountain on the Bataan Peninsula where shy Negritos still live in the forest recesses.

3. Language

THE PACIFIC PEOPLES have a Babel of local languages and dialects. But under the influences of modern trade and travel, and through the activities of governments and missions, a handful of tongues has become widely used. Even a little understanding of these common forms of speech will take the visitor a long way. A considerable number of natives, too, are by now able to speak the language of the governing group,—that is, English, Dutch, or French,—and many can read and write at least in their local tongues. This is particularly true of groups living around the port centers and of the young people who have been to school.

Even when words fail because of language limitations, the visitor may still be able to get his points across. He has his voice to make expressive sounds, and also his face, hands, and body with which to make signs and demonstrate his meanings in pantomime. He can also use pencil and paper, or draw pictures on the ground with a stick.

THE NATIVE LANGUAGES

Language experts trace most of the native languages spoken in Malaysia and Oceania back to a common origin, so that they form a great "family" of related languages. To this language family is given the name Austronesian ("southern island") or Malayo-Polynesian. Included in it are all the dozen or so Polynesian dialects such as Samoan, Hawaiian and Maori, all those of Micronesia, numbering some fifteen, all the hundreds of languages and dialects of the Malaysian peoples, and many of the numerous tongues used in Melanesia, especially along the east coasts of New Guinea and in the island chains eastward from here to Fiji. Speech of the Austronesian stock is even found farther west across the Indian Ocean in Madagascar, the so-called Malagasy. Clearly it has been a language type of maritime peoples who have carried it far and wide from the southeast Asian area.

These languages as found today have a rather similar grammatical form and sound system, and even their vocabularies usually have a good many words in common in spite of the hundreds of years during which they have been developing along different lines. Basic words such as those for fire, water, canoe, house, and coconut tree are much the same from one side of the area to the other.

In the New Guinea region and in Australia this pattern of related languages is broken by what are evidently pockets of old languages, brought in by the early peoples settling in those areas. All too little is known about these tongues. Their number appears to run into hundreds, and in some parts of the region almost every bay, valley, and hilltop has its own distinctive speech. Such languages show no relation to the Austronesian family, and often none at all to one another, so great are the local differences that have come about with long isolation. Usually those in the New Guinea region are grouped for convenience under the name "Papuan." They occur as far west as Halmahera in the Moluccas, also in western and inland New Guinea, and here and there in the Bismarcks and other more easterly groups. The dozens of languages in Australia are given the general name "Australian." The few Westerners who have learned languages of these types report that they are grammatically complicated and difficult—anything but the simple speech which might be expected among such peoples.

MODERN LANGUAGE CHANGES

Languages grow and change in these island areas, just as western speech is doing constantly by way of the scientific laboratory, theater, and other creative influences. The islanders have not only modified their own speech materials to fit new experience but also have taken over words and ideas from every outside people with whom they have come into contact.

Centuries back, the languages of the western Pacific were influenced in this way by Indian Sanskrit, by Chinese, and by Arabic, sacred language of the Koran. Later, words and ideas were adopted from Portuguese, Spanish, English, French, and other western tongues. The traveler will come across many familiar terms being used in the native speech, from airplane to zoo. But he may find difficulty at first in picking them up, because the local people give them a native style pronunciation. Christmas, for instance, may sound like "Kelisimasi" and box like "pokis." The Japanese have adopted several thousand English words in this way, and English itself is a museum of many languages as a result of similar word borrowing. Natives, especially around the ports, often use an amazing jumble of mixed talk.

The visitor may want to learn something of the local speech if he stays in one place for any length of time, for the people will use it among themselves in carrying on their daily life. But he must not expect it to carry him far. On another island across a few miles of water, or three villages down the coast, it may be hardly understood. What is worth the effort of learning as fully as possible is any common language or *lingua franca* which has become widely current in the area.

COMMON LANGUAGES

Even before the whites came, native groups who did much trading with one another usually found it useful to learn a

Royal Dutch Packet Navigation Co. and Netherlands Information Bureau

PLATE 7

Upper. The Borobudhur—gigantic and beautiful Buddhist shrine in central Java. Along its galleries bas-reliefs describing the life of Buddha run for about three and a half miles.

Lower. The social system and the arts of Java today keep alive much of the old "Indo-Malayan" civilization. An aristocratic Javanese audience here watches masked dancers in a performance depicting the tradition and history of earlier days.

U.S. Marine Corps and Press

PLATE 8

Upper. Friendliness is a universal language, as marines found in the Solomons.

Lower. Making friends with the children is always interesting and also helps in establishing good relations with the adults. Young New Caledonians show how fish are shot with bow and arrow.

common speech in addition to their own, generally that of the group which was most active in the trading business. Later when white traders, missionaries, and officials arrived, these newcomers encouraged the spread of some general medium of communication through which they could get into touch with the natives over a large region without learning all the local varieties of speech.

A common language coin of this kind is not usually hard to learn. The islanders pick it up quickly without ever going to school. It may be based upon a native language, but if so it is generally simplified and then embroidered with many useful additions from outside speech. Nearly always the basic native tongue involved will be that of the port area where trade has been most concentrated or where white visitors first came. Thus *pasar Malay* ("bazaar" or market Malay) spread from the ports of Malacca and Batavia to become the *lingua franca* of millions in Dutch and British areas of Malaysia. *Motu,* speech of the Port Moresby district in Papua, was the basis for the common tongue now used in that territory. Alternatively, such a general language may be built upon a western rather than a native tongue. This is true of the so-called "pidgin" ("business") languages of the China coast and of the Pacific islands, comprising various simplified forms of Portuguese, Spanish, French, and English.

The best-known type is probably the so-called "pidgin-English" of the South Seas. This took form out of the lusty talk of early sailors and traders, combined with the simple English vocabulary which the natives picked up informally. Known originally as *bêche-de-mer* ("sea-slug") or Sandalwood-English because of its association with early commerce in these products, it has developed into two main types of dialects—New Guinea pidgin in the west, and Solomons pidgin in the Solomons-New Hebrides area. Its jargon form may easily deceive the newcomer into thinking that all he has to do is to slur or simplify his English in order to be understood. In actual fact the special grammar and vocabulary of pidgin has to be carefully learned and rigidly followed in speaking. Along with English it contains words from native languages, Malay, Portuguese, German, and other tongues. Its grammar is basically Melanesian, and natives give it their own varying local pronunciations. The China coast pidgin is very different, as is also the "bamboo-English" of the Philippines, a simplified form of American speech with a Filipino accent. In the French colonies pidgin-French has its local varieties.

The New Guinea region is probably the most complicated language area to be found in the world today. In addition to the numerous native tongues it has a variety of common languages used in different localities and sometimes even in the same place. Some are products of centuries-old native trading, as already described; others are of modern origin. Each of the mission bodies, Catholic and Protestant, British, American, French, and German, usually took a native language of the particular district in which its work was concentrated and made it into a common tongue through which its converts could read the Bible and carry on religious services. Natives who went to the higher mission schools might also be taught some English, French, or German. Added to these are the principal trade tongues, New Guinea pidgin in the mandated territory and Motu in Papua. Finally, a small number of educated natives, usually persons in government service, can speak regular English quite well.

The Philippines, too, have a complicated language problem. Out of some eighty local languages and dialects, three became widely spoken as common languages during Spanish days— Tagalog in the central region around the capital city of Manila, Ilocano in the north, and Visayan in the south. The more educated Filipino might know something of all three, as well as some Spanish. Then after the coming of the Americans, English was widely taught in the schools and was made the official common speech. Recently the Philippine Commonwealth government put on top the final coping stone of language by deciding that a modified form of Tagalog, speech of Manila, was to become the national tongue.

The Japanese mandated islands had no over-all common tongue above their local Micronesian dialects before the Japanese went into the area. By now, however, the younger people can usually speak Japanese, at least in simplified form. In the western part of the mandate (the Marianas, western Carolines, and Palaus) many natives use the Chamorro language, which is also the speech of the people in American Guam. As many of the Guam people are able to speak excellent English, they may be of help to military personnel or civilians wanting to get into touch with the natives of these neighboring islands. In the Japanese mandate a scattering of natives and part-natives, especially among the older generation, can speak some English, German, or Spanish.

LANGUAGE LEARNING

A notebook and pencil are virtually essential in getting to know a new language. If the visitor finds himself in an area for which he has no dictionaries or other materials on the local speech, he can undertake the fascinating task of recording it for himself. To make a start, he might point to a button on his coat, say to a native, "Button," and then point to some object on the native's person with an enquiring "Huh?" The native will soon catch on, and very quickly a good start will have been made with collecting the local word-tickets.

Learning a language, however, is much more than a matter of tuning the ear to catch words correctly, or of knowing how speech is put together grammatically. A close eye should be kept, too, on facial expressions and on movements of the hands, arms, and body which may be just as much a part of language as the spoken word. The local terms and gestures connected with etiquette are especially worth learning, for these are just as highly important to native peoples as they are in white society.

The native equivalents of "Good-day," "Thank you," a handshake, and other courtesies will carry a stranger far in developing friendliness and trust. Native languages are likely to have special "honorific" terms which are used in addressing important persons in order to pay respect to their status, and these are also useful to know. A visitor can make a fair showing with a native language by mastering a few hundred words; indeed, the average English-speaking person uses most of the time only three or four thousand words out of the hundreds of thousands in the English dictionary.

One of the most interesting things about language in places like the Pacific islands is how far a person may get along without it. Where verbal understanding fails, he can think himself back to the old days of movie silents. Facial expressions, gestures, and pantomime, accompanied by appropriate sound effects, should take him a long way, and as noted previously, drawings may also be used. A wide friendly smile, empty raised hands, and a firm confident poise, have saved the lives of many government officials and other travelers when they encountered isolated peoples who had never seen a white man before. Natives are quick to read from the tone of voice and the manner of a stranger whether he is friend or enemy, sure of himself or afraid. They readily sense contemptuous or other derogatory talk about them, or a joke at their expense, even though they may understand no word of what is being said—a fact to be careful about. In the same way an outsider should be able to get the gist of what natives are thinking if he watches their faces and gestures carefully.

USING INTERPRETERS

A note of warning is in order to those who have to use natives as interpreters, even when such individuals know English well. They should always keep a question-mark in their minds about information secured through an interpreter until it has been carefully checked. There is a constant danger that such material will be distorted, even if not intentionally, in passing through the mind of an intermediary. Watching an interpreter's face, and repeating a question after letting an interval pass, are among the methods of weighing how far he may be intruding his own ideas. The fact that a native is being used by a white man in this way gives him a tremendous prestige in the eyes of his fellows, and there is a strong temptation for him to twist both ends of a conversation to his own advantage, or to please both parties. Corresponding safeguards, indeed, must be exercised as regards any native informant.

LITERACY

Most dealings with the islanders will have to be carried on through personal contact and by word of mouth. Except around the few large cities the islands would not offer any sort of living for radio announcers or newspaper columnists. Nevertheless many natives have by now become literate in their own tongues, and an increasing number are able to read and write the common languages such as pidgin, and even English, Dutch, or French.

Most native villages today have one or more persons—native officials, mission pastors, or school graduates—who can understand written messages. Where school systems and Christian missions have been established for any length of time, a large part or even all of the population may be literate. In the Gilbert Islands, for instance, virtually one hundred per cent of the natives are able to read and write at least in the Gilbertese language. In developed areas such as Java and the Philippines, numerous native language newspapers and periodicals are published, and everywhere government and mission presses issue materials in the more important local languages. In the Mohammedan regions, persons who can read the sacred Arabic language are treated with great respect.

4. Government

POLITICALLY THE ISLANDS of the Pacific form a strange patchwork. Annexed by the interested powers primarily for their strategic importance, they are broken up into twenty-six separate units, including colonies, territories, protectorates, and mandates. These are held today by nine different nations—Australia, Chile, France, Great Britain, Holland, Japan, New Zealand, Portugal, and the United States. Two other nations formerly had stakes in the area, and leave their marks—Spain and Germany. This island region is one of the great colonial zones of the earth, and the local peoples, whether they like it or not, are under the control of alien outsiders.

Westerners are used to living in a country where all local groups, however different they may be, and proud as they may feel about their own towns and districts, are linked together as citizens of a nation. In these Pacific areas such political consolidation, which indeed is one of the more recent inventions of human civilization, has as yet made little headway. The people still live in small, more or less independent groups, and their thinking is almost wholly in local terms. This helps to explain why outside nations could take control of their territories so easily. Even in these days of peace and safe travel, most natives dislike leaving their ancestral localities, and may easily become lost outside their own districts.

Some political consolidation has taken place, it is true. Mention has already been made of the states and empires which arose in the western Pacific during earlier centuries, and of the three hundred or so native states existing today within the structures of modern government. In the South Seas, too, a number of native "kings" emerged in the early days of white contact, using guns to conquer their neighbors and patterning their thrones on those of European monarchs. A few of these native rulers have survived the annexations of later years, notably in Tonga where a regal Polynesian Queen, Salote (Charlotte), reigns under British protection. For the most part, however, the overlordship of sultan, rajah, or native monarch is a ceremonious and shadowy thing so far as the ordinary people are concerned.

So, too, are the newer political loyalties to the extent that they have been developed by native groups in relation to their British, Dutch, or other rulers. The colonial holdings which have been carved out by the great powers are almost without exception highly artificial units taking in many formerly independent and diversified native groups. Only slowly is a sense of identity and loyalty developing in relation to these units—a feeling of being an Indonesian, a Solomon Islander, or a Fijian. As would be expected, this sense of belonging grows about proportionately to the degree of education the people have received, and to the extent that communications have been developed. A group such as the population of the Philippines is therefore much further along in the welding process than the average. The typical islander, however, is still first and foremost a man of his kin group and village. Above these familiar units the superimposed political layers of modern colonialism fade into the mists of indifference if not of ignorance.

From the practical viewpoint this means that each native community has to be treated as a unit more or less on its own. Where in a western nation the country as a whole may be reached immediately by some government order given via the press or radio, here first-hand contact must usually be established with each separate district or even village, either directly or by messengers. In turn, within a community, the most effective contact is through personal relations with its political leaders, the men of authority who control and direct its largely self-contained life.

CENTRAL GOVERNMENT

The typical Pacific island jurisdiction of today is headed by a governor or administrator who rules with pomp yet efficiency on behalf of his home government. Under him are executive departments to deal with local affairs such as finance, public works, health, and labor. He receives some of his orders from the home country, but he is also aided and advised in legislative matters by local councils containing representatives of the white residents and perhaps of the natives and other population groups. Regional government within each territory is carried on by district officers or magistrates, aided by mobile patrol officers who make the rounds of local communities.

How far the native peoples take part in such administrative systems depends upon their degree of political development and especially upon the colonial philosophy and policy of the controlling imperial power. Very great differences are found from place to place, but the general trend is away from the absolutism of earlier colonial days and toward allowing the local peoples greater training and opportunities in government.

In all administrations, trained natives have been given an increasing number of the less responsible executive positions, being used as minor officials, clerks, teachers, radio operators, mechanics, and in many other tasks. A few governments now put natives in top positions such as department heads, though usually with white helpers continuing at their elbows as "elder brothers" to guide them. In the Philippines, however, official posts from top to bottom are in Filipino hands. This native personnel in government forms something of a new aristocracy, especially in the cities and towns, and native families may strain their resources to send a youth through the higher schools so that he may become eligible for a government post. Part-natives are also usually well represented in this group.

On the legislative side the native peoples in some jurisdictions have been allowed representation right up to the highest councils of the central government. In the Volksraad, or "People's Council" of the Netherlands Indies, a body enjoying a considerable degree of legislative power, thirty of the sixty members have been Indonesians, these partly appointed by the government and partly elected by regional councils. Instead of, or along with such a mixed council in which native representatives sit together with those of other population groups, some administrations have set up a purely native council to give advice on native matters. Examples of such native bodies are the "Great Council of Chiefs" in Fiji and the *Fono* (Council or Circle) of representatives in Samoa. In Guam a Congress with two Houses follows American patterns but has only advisory powers. Tonga has an Assembly made up equally of elected representatives of the "nobles" or aristocratic families and of the "commoners."

In some territories native representation is limited to local councils dealing with district and village affairs. In the Gilbert and Ellice Islands colony each little island has its own elected council, together with its own native officials and courts, so that it is practically self-governing; local affairs are merely subject to review by white administrators on their periodic visits. At the bottom of the scale of modern political development are the New Guinea territories, the Solomons, and the New Hebrides, where the native peoples have no legislative representation. Even here, however, the government authorities keep in touch as closely as possible with the ideas of the people through local native officials and traditional community councils.

On the judicial side, native magistrates and courts may be used to deal with the less serious crimes and misdemeanors; or at least native leaders may be appointed to sit with whites on the bench, or may be invited to act as advisers. The great advantage here is that such individuals know the native mind and custom. The white administrator is better able to avoid getting the government into trouble through making decisions which the native people consider unjust. Except in the semi-independent Philippines, however, the more lusty crimes go before the white man's bar of justice.

One of the most extraordinarily successful aspects of administration has been the enlistment of natives in police or constabulary forces. At times these men may come from remote villages only recently broken in to western control. Carefully selected and trained, put into uniforms which the visitor soon learns to recognize in the different jurisdictions, and led by a handful of white officers, they have perhaps been the most influential agents in bringing law and order to the outer regions of the island world. On any expedition involving difficult terrain, contact with new native groups, procuring emergency foods, or learning about enemy movements, a person can count himself lucky if he has one or more of these police "boys" along. The white administrators in most areas would be lost without the loyal service of these remarkable men.

LOCAL GOVERNMENT

Except in the remote uncontrolled fastnesses of the New Guinea region, any native settlement will have certain leaders who are used to handling business with visiting whites. Any reasonably large settlement, too, is sure to have native officials who are in the regular government service, such as a headman or mayor, an interpreter or scribe who understands the common speech of the region and probably can write, and perhaps others such as a village policeman and a medical orderly. These are nearly always local persons, though in more backward areas a district official may be a picked native from some outside place.

In Fiji, Samoa, and certain other jurisdictions the governments have created women's committees in the more accessible villages to deal with health and child welfare matters.

The exact names given to local officials, and the duties they perform, vary in the different jurisdictions. Some may be appointed directly by the government, others elected by the community under official supervision. Their tenure of office may be for a fixed or for an indefinite period. A stranger going into any district should find out beforehand what the system is, and if possible the personal characteristics and the reliability of the local officials. He should also know how such persons may be recognized, so that he can distinguish the headman, the policeman, and others. They are the key people to approach for getting anything done.

The visitor may not be particularly impressed at his first sight of local native officials. Their only marks may be an official cap or coat with buttons, sometimes faded and dirty, or a badge, a cane, or a whistle. In some places the headman may be a rather shifty individual, put into his position because of his native-style importance, and he may try to exploit an outsider for his own purposes; after all, he is a man of his village first, and an official of the government second. Yet often such officials are amazingly competent, and the people will usually spring into action at their word.

COMMUNITY LAW AND ORDER

Each native settlement tends to be a self-governing unit so far as its internal affairs are concerned. However rudimentary may be the knowledge of the people regarding western political institutions and ideals, they are competent enough in carrying on the traditional methods of order and control. Local usages differ, but nearly always a community is run by a consulting group of the local elders or heads of families more or less formally organized into a council. Usually the members are men, but women of importance may have a strong voice, and there may be a parallel women's group to supervise exclusively female affairs.

A visitor present at a community council can begin finding out who the members are and what their relative authority and say in the council is; the group will be a sort of local "Who's Who." They may be the senior members of households or of clans; some may be important because of aristocratic birth, or accumulation of ceremonial wealth, or expertness in things supernatural. Nowadays any persons vested with government authority usually have a major voice, particularly if they are important in their own right as members of the community.

Such a consulting group of leading people generally manages to run local affairs smoothly for the very good reason that the members are the expert interpreters of the ancestral traditions and the customary law, often called by its Malay name *adat*. Some theorists have put forward the mistaken idea that primitive peoples have no law, or that they hew to the line of custom because of supernatural fears or slavish habits. It is true that they rarely have anything exactly corresponding to policemen, judges, and jails. Yet each group has its well-formulated system of rules, of "do's" and "don'ts" by which life is regulated—an oral if not a written code. It also has powerful influences which cause members to conform to the rules, and methods of trial and punishment to deal with law-breakers.

As in communities the world over, the pressure of public opinion is a tremendously strong force in getting people to keep to the local customs, and in ostracizing those who refuse to conform. In these intimate societies there are big dividends of social approval and material gain for the person who will fit in, and heavy penalties for the delinquent. Such forces have been the more powerful because until recently the non-conformist could not, as in a large western country, escape them by moving somewhere else to live. To do so might mean certain death from warlike neighbors. The local rules receive the backing of religious "sanctions" and the more important ones become taboos; that is, the person breaking them must expect direct reprisals from supernatural forces. A Westerner may understand better the obedience of natives to local custom if he asks why he himself, without being in danger of arrest from a policeman, keeps the festival of Christmas, salutes the flag, and does not interrupt a prayer during church service.

The judge-and-jury aspect of law is usually provided in these little groups by family and community councils sitting in a judicial capacity. Sometimes supernatural judgments are invoked, as through ordeals such as plunging a hand into boiling water, or examining the entrails of a sacrificed animal to read the opinion of the deities, or in a Christianized group swearing on the Bible. Faced with the prospect of such a test, a wrongdoer usually confesses.

Western governments, and also mission bodies, have inevitably upset in some degree these local systems of law and order. They have curbed the powers of local leaders, and have introduced new codes regarding property, relations with neighboring groups, marriage, burial, and many other matters. To the extent that these new rules go against the traditional native usages, the native finds himself put into the uncertain position of being a law-breaker whether he sticks to his own tenets or obeys those of the white man. An individual may be basking in community approval for some act which is honorable by local custom, only to have the government authorities step in and carry him off to jail. His only consolation may be that his fellows regard him as a martyr instead of a criminal.

Even greater trouble may come from the fact that a native, dissatisfied by rulings he gets from the elders on property questions or other disputed matters, is tempted to take his case to the white man's bar of justice. Or if members of the community inflict a native-style punishment he may try to get his own back by bringing charges against them. The dockets of district officers and similar white officials have become increasingly crowded with disputes over land, succession, inheritance, marital relations, and other concerns which would formerly have been settled by the customary law, or alternately by the grim "arbitration" of fighting and feuding. This happens most extensively in communities undergoing rapid change, such as those around the ports and industrial centers.

Military personnel as well as civilian officials may find themselves called upon to settle delicate questions of this kind. To do so requires not only the wisdom of a Solomon but also a penetrating knowledge of native customs. Without meaning to, or possibly without being aware of it, a Westerner may have his brand of justice exploited for devious native ends, and a wrong decision may arouse the wrath of powerful native groups or the opposition of the elders. Experienced administrators have learned to tread gingerly and warily in this field of native law, and in imposing western codes upon such groups or interfering with the traditional powers of their leaders.

A visitor from democratic countries is particularly interested in how far native institutions are flavored with the democratic spirit, or are capable of being remodeled toward the forms of democracy. Some island groups already show a strong emphasis of this kind, talking matters out in family and community meetings in which everyone may have a say.

Other groups, however, have marked class or other distinctions which make the word of certain individuals much more influential than that of others. Democratic methods which give an equal vote to a sultan or chief and a nobody are here likely to be resisted by conservatives, especially the important people, even while such ways may be increasingly welcomed by the educated youth and by the nobodies. The idea of counting votes may itself be foreign to peoples who are used to talking out any important question until a unanimous opinion is reached, since their intimate little communities can hardly bear the strain of any public majority-minority lineup. Here democratic methods will become soundly rooted only through the long pull of political education.

THE NATIVE STATES

In earlier days the imperial nations brought under direct government rule some of the more troublesome native realms. But for the most part they found it expedient to make treaties with the local rulers so that their states came within the framework of modern administration as "protectorates" or "self-governing territories." These treaties usually specified that the white authorities would respect local religious and other customs, and that the native rulers would in turn accept the "advice" of representatives of the protecting powers.

In actual practice the tendency has been for the native states, while remaining autonomous in formal terms, to become meshed in with the general administration. Before the war, white Advisers or Residents diplomatically shaped the essential policies of the state. Sultans and rajahs kept up the colorful pomp of their thrones and courts, yet on the practical side they had become more like high civil service officers. Nearly always the revenues and services which their subjects formerly gave to them personally went instead to the state treasury, from which they drew a fixed salary. The rulers would still have around them retinues of court officials such as viziers or prime ministers, and state councils on which local notables had the right to sit and so get their traditional status and prestige recognized. But behind these ceremonious façades the affairs of government were likely to be run unobtrusively by a group of trained civil service officers, mostly natives of the area but including whites in key posts.

Netherlands Information Bureau

PLATE 9

Pasar Malay developed as a language of the market place. The "pasar" at Pajacombo in west Sumatra.

U.S. Marine

PLATE 10

Gestures and signs will carry on where language fails. These Solomon Island children take the chance to do a little business.

NATIONALISM

The political competence of these island peoples, and their fitness for modern-style self-government, have been the subject of much discussion and controversy. In recent years movements akin to what is popularly called "nationalism" have been stirring in many of the colonial areas. These are strongest in the large dependencies of the western Pacific which have had long contact with western civilization, such as the Netherlands Indies, the Philippines, and Indochina, but they are also emerging in smaller places like Samoa and Fiji. At their van are some of the more educated native and part-native leaders. Though as yet their followings are rarely large proportionate to the total numbers in the areas concerned, such movements are of great significance. They arise from the same atmosphere of emotional tension as that which existed in the American colonies before the Revolution.

In the nineteenth and early twentieth centuries, influential natives began to emerge here and there in Malaysia and elsewhere, calling upon their peoples to prepare themselves to stand upon their own feet politically and culturally. Probably the outstanding figure to date has been José Rizal, Filipino hero and martyr who was shot in 1896 by a Spanish firing squad. Doctor, lawyer, artist, writer, in fact a sort of Malaysian Leonardo da Vinci, he has been the Sun Yat-sen of the modern Philippines. One of the early leaders in Java was a Javanese woman, Princess Kartini, who died at the age of twenty-four after launching educational and other activities among women and children. Nationalist organizations mushroomed, especially among the western-educated "intellectuals" and students, but also drawing support from workers in the towns, from Islamic religious groups, and to some extent from rural peasants and tenants.

So long as these organizations concerned themselves with

cultural and welfare activities they received the blessing of colonial governments. In Java, for example, old arts and crafts were revived, and nationalist schools, study clubs, and medical centers were founded. Usually, too, the authorities permitted orderly political parties to be formed, so that native seats in any legislative bodies were contested by candidates from these parties just as with the legislatures of western countries. But the nationalists went further by trying to organize labor and to attack the economic status quo. They also demanded much greater rights of self-government, and some leaders and parties demanded complete and immediate independence.

In the Philippines the American government met this request by initiating a transitional period of "trial independence" which was to have been completed in 1946 but was interrupted by the Japanese attack. Other colonial authorities have taken a more conservative stand, looking rather toward the development of self-government and "partnership" within the existing imperial framework. On occasions they have suppressed nationalist organizations and imprisoned or banished their leaders. A number of serious outbreaks have occurred and blood has been shed, especially in Indochina and Java.

Nationalist leaders have claimed that they could run their countries at least as well as the alien administrators from outside. But the imperial authorities have countered by insisting that fuller self-government could only be given as the mass of the people gradually became competent and the heterogeneous population groups became consolidated. They have also pointed to the entrenched stakes of non-native populations in these areas, requiring security and consideration. The extreme nationalist sentiment reached its height in these countries from 1924 to 1931, but fell away considerably during the next decade as the Japanese tides of aggression began to engulf the Orient.

Colonial authorities have generally attributed the growth of aggressive nationalist spirit to communist influences. It is true that communist organizers played some part in Malaysia, especially in the period up to 1931. But such movements arise essentially out of strains and stresses in the local setting. Above all, perhaps, there is the humiliation and frustration that people feel in having their lives dominated by outsiders who count themselves superior. Contact of the educated people with western ideas of liberty and equality is another potent ferment. Depressed economic and social conditions, the draining away of local resources through alien exploitation, social discrimination by whites against natives, and a growing disillusionment among these peoples as regards the omnipotence of western civilization, are among other elements which stir the native mind. They may be found in island communities that have never heard of a communist.

In earlier days, the natural reaction of native groups was to try to drive out the white man. The frontier record is full of "revolts" and "uprisings," and such a pattern of reaction still occurs at times in recently pacified zones of the Melanesian region. These outbreaks are, of course, forcibly suppressed, as has been done in the past. The native peoples concerned are then likely to retreat into an attitude of conservatism, if not of sullenness or even of hopelessness. Alternatively they may bolster their morale through compensatory activities such as clinging deliberately to their own traditional customs, wearing gaudy clothes, adopting a chip-on-the-shoulder or devil-may-care attitude, or drinking excessively. Some find solace and escape in the spiritual promises of the church, or in often fantastic doctrines of native cults, mystical movements, or secret societies.

By no means all groups or individuals swing to these more extreme types of outlet. Yet everywhere native minds tend to be stirred with a vague malaise and uncertainty in the face of the new order. The nationalist leader who reaches back to harness these emotional tensions can usually get an enthusiastic if not always politically intelligent following. Such conditions are by no means confined to native groups, but also show in western communities with the rapid changes of modern days.

No strong current of political nationalism in the modern sense is to be expected as yet in such a politically fragmented region as Melanesia. At most it is vaguely touching some of the youth around the ports and towns. But in places like Java, with a long tradition of political solidarity, perhaps a "golden age" of earlier imperial greatness to dwell upon in retrospect, and thousands of educated and politically minded persons, it is a factor to be reckoned with. The visitor going into such areas faces a delicate and somewhat tense situation. In the longer distance view this problem of native aspirations in such colonial areas is one of the most difficult yet hopeful that international peacemakers must face.

THE POLITICAL FUTURE

A major country such as the Philippines may justly aspire to autonomy on the world stage; it is much larger than a number of the European nations. Nearly all the present colonial units, however, are far too small for this. Unless gradually welded together into some form of island federation, or caught into a new international structure, they must remain within the orbit of an outside power. A factor of importance here is the strategic position of the islands in relation to Pacific and world security.

Even though such smaller colonial units may not achieve a separate political identity, their local peoples may nevertheless look forward to autonomy in their internal affairs. The future will doubtless see these peoples developing and changing their traditional institutions to fit modern ideas of government, and working out a sense of unity among their hitherto scattered groups. Those more advanced in this process such as the Filipinos and Tongans demonstrate that this is fully possible. The political destiny of the islanders, however, depends in its broader outlines upon the decisions made by the great powers as regards the disposition of colonial areas and the building of international structures which may take responsibilities toward such smaller peoples.

5. Livelihood

THE GREAT MAJORITY of the islanders today live close to the soil and sea, as did their ancestors. Even those located in the relatively few cities and towns or at plantation and mining centers, usually try to follow as far as possible their traditional diet and economic habits. Unless required by their employers to live in town or in labor barracks, they mostly leave the main centers to the whites, Chinese, or other non-native peoples, preferring to stay a little way out in more open country. Away from these few places, native groups continue to win a livelihood much as in the past.

A closer look, however, will show that certain changes have taken place. The people have usually taken over some new plants and animals from the outside world—corn, perhaps, from America and horses from Europe. Almost everywhere, too, they have learned to depend upon the trading store or market for new articles such as matches, iron tools, and cloth. In turn they have to produce goods which the trader will take, or sell their labor to raise money. Rarely, however, do the islanders think that the white man has many new tricks to teach them, other than what they have already elected to take over for themselves from western civilization. People do not easily change their habits as regards food and other essentials for physical survival.

In such an island setting there is considerable truth in their point of view. On a barren atoll, for instance, the main reaction of a visitor may be one of astonishment that anyone could manage even to survive there permanently. Then, as he sees the sturdy physique and good teeth of the local natives he will realize that their diet must be adequate. Following up the matter, he will note that they not only use all available land foods, but also exploit intensively the animal and vegetable life of the lagoon and ocean—a kind of marine farming. The conclusion may well be drawn that, apart from control of any new pests and plant diseases which may offer a threat, there is little the white expert can teach the islanders about how to manage in such a setting.

The same would be true of many groups who live in swamp country, in deep forests, or on barren mountain slopes of the high interior. They have their special kinds of local resources around which their economic life is built. The only alternative to carrying on the traditional round in the same basic way would probably be to leave their ancestral homes and come out to what seem by the white man's standards to be more hospitable regions. Yet if they were asked, the reply of nearly everyone would be an emphatic "No."

By no means all the islanders, of course, have such restrictive settings for their lives. In river valleys and along the less swampy coastal flats on the higher islands the soil is often quite rich. In some places, active volcanoes renew the soil by casting out rock and ash that are particularly fertile, as in Java and around Rabaul. Even when the soil is poor, as it often may be because of the leaching effect of heavy tropical rains, it may produce well if fertilized and irrigated or if the land is left fallow for long periods between crops. Where a coastal district has a reef and lagoon, or sheltered seas, the people can get plentiful marine resources to diversify their economic base. Products of inland lakes and rivers may also be drawn upon by the local peoples.

Groups living in such places have more elbow room for winning a livelihood. They have often been able to choose between different lines of economic development—whether to stress agriculture, industry, fishing, hunting, or gathering forest products. In western Malaysia a people such as the Javanese are able to support a population numbering millions by intensive cultivation of rice and other high-yield crops, by small handicraft industries, and by fishing and raising fish in artificial ponds. At the other extreme, native groups in many parts of the New Guinea-Solomons area use their land and other resources meagerly. Here populations are sparse, and there is great room for economic improvement.

The native who lives in the cities and towns often has a lower scale of living than the rural native. A small proportion of such people hold superior positions, with what by native standards is a good income, as for example government officials in the higher brackets, teachers, clerks, skilled artisans, and "boss boys" or foremen. Richer natives such as landlords and aristocrats may also live in town. But by far the majority are likely to be low-paid workers often getting only casual employment as stevedores, street cleaners, house servants, factory hands, and pullers and carriers of heavy loads. Where there are factories, notably in city centers like Batavia and Manila, large numbers of native women may be employed, thus supplementing small family incomes.

Since early days, such urban centers have been like magnets drawing in natives from the outer areas. Here have come the ambitious, the discontented, the rubbernecking bumpkins, and the very poor. As all have wanted jobs to maintain themselves, and the opportunities are limited, unemployment has been increasing. Plenty of natives are always to be seen loitering around the streets or lining up at any charity and relief centers. Natives are constantly coming and going, many of course returning unhappy to their home communities because they have not made fortunes. Nearly always any native who has a good home and a steady job has a group of poorer relatives gathered around his kitchen and backyard. As Allied forces drive out

R. H. Beck, Matson Navigation Co., and Netherlands Information Bureau

PLATE 11

Upper. A Fijian village. The local community, with its busy and largely self-sufficient life, is still the basic unit of island affairs.

Lower left. King Kalakaua of Hawaii. In early days, native kings arose, like European monarchs. Except in Tonga and a few other islands, they have disappeared.

Lower right. The Sultan of Jogjakarta, Java, in official costume, accompanied by his Dutch "elder brother," the Governor of the State.

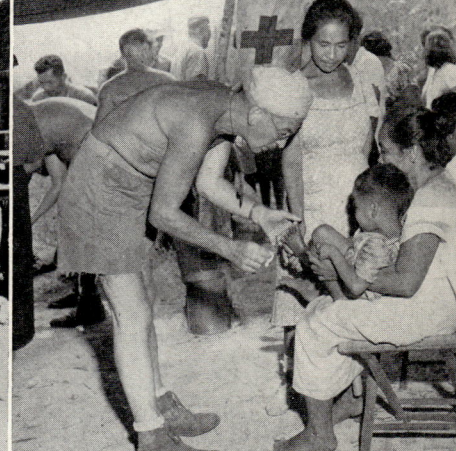

U.S. Marine Corps and Press

PLATE 12

Upper. A detachment of the Samoan Marine Battalion in American Samoa is inspected by Lieutenant General A. A. Vandergrift.

Lower left. The Royal Armed Papuan Constabulary has been the backbone of law and order in that territory for more than half a century.

Lower right. A Chamorro nurse, formerly attached to the U.S. Naval Hospital in Guam, helps an American doctor when our troops reoccupy that island.

Wallace Adams Collection, American Museum of Natural History and Netherlands Information Bureau

PLATE 13

Upper. Terraced rice fields reach their greatest development among the mountain peoples of the northern Philippines.

Lower. Water-buffaloes are used to prepare the rice fields in western Malaysia.

Netherlands Information Bureau, Pan Pacific and American Museum of Natural H

PLATE 14

Upper. Fishing craft of various types at Grissee in east Java.

Lower left. Polynesian fishermen carry their outrigger canoe up the beach.

Lower right. Making "shell money" in the Solomons. The string of shell discs is given its final polishing with sand and water and a stone to even the edges. This is at Auki on the coast of Malaita.

the Japanese from the occupied areas it will be these city masses who will be most in need of relief, not the rural people.

Another large class of natives who are away from their home villages are the laborers at plantations and mines. Frequently they have indentured themselves to their employers for a period of months or years, and so cannot leave without going to prison for breach of contract. With Chinese, Indian, and other laborers they may live in barracks or "labor lines," or they may be permitted to set up small huts of their own. Most laborers do not have their wives and families with them. Their employers usually issue food rations which are fixed by government regulations, but alternatively the laborers may be given a money allowance for food. These workers may do a little gardening and fishing outside of work hours, but mostly they live on store foods, as do the townspeople. Many thousands of such laborers were caught far from their home districts at the time of the Japanese attack. In the New Guinea mandate, where almost one quarter of the adult male natives were under indenture, many probably lost their lives in trying to make their way home through the territories of strange tribes.

NATIVE ECONOMIC SYSTEMS

Very great differences are found from place to place in what the island peoples count as "wealth," what wants they have that lead them to expend effort. One group may concentrate its major attention upon a particular agricultural crop, such as rice. Life for such a people becomes a kind of drama centered around the busy cycle from one harvest to the next. Another group may seem to count it the most exciting thing in life to own strings of "shell-money," old porcelain ware, ornaments of precious metals and precious stones, or other ceremonial objects. What are usually thought of as "standards of living" may vary greatly according to the values that people put upon different types of goods and activities. The white man's yardsticks of economic worth—a bank account, up-to-date plumbing, an automobile, and whatever else one might want to add—would cause hardly a ripple of interest in some of these societies. They measure the "good life" in very different terms, which may have little appeal to the white man.

The islanders also organize their economic affairs in amazingly different ways. As in the western economic system, their goods have to be produced; they are also distributed, owned, and used or "consumed." But in all this there may be the greatest range from rugged individualism and competition far beyond that characteristic even of go-getting Americans, to group cooperation and "collectivism." In some groups a person is encouraged to accumulate extensive wealth for himself in order to become important, but in others this would be regarded as immoral, or almost inconceivable. According to the economic philosophy of the latter people, the individual joins effort with his kinsmen and neighbors for their common support, and gets his personal glory from doing his share as efficiently as he can. Nearly always, however, in these societies as in western countries, the every-day working group is a household or small unit of people that lives and eats under one roof.

Invariably an intimate connection exists between the important economic activities and the local religion. Producing the staple foods, building houses, making canoes, and everything else vital to survival and welfare are saturated with religious ideas and rituals. After all, it is here that people undergo many of their greatest anxieties and uncertainties, and therefore seek the help of spiritual forces as they interpret them. Growing a seasonal crop like rice or yams becomes a main basis for the local religious calendar, ending of course with a thanksgiving "harvest festival," as western churches do back home. A coastal people has many kinds of magical rites, charms, and taboos which in their eyes are just as vital to a fishing expedition as taking along lines and nets. Peoples may have religious prohibitions against eating or interfering with certain types of plants and animals.

Close links also exist between economic matters and the local social system. A chief or aristocrat may build up his status and prestige by accumulating special kinds of ceremonial property, or giving huge feasts, or passing out ostentatiously large amounts of valuables. His kinsmen and supporters may correspondingly be required by custom to give him tribute and services so that he can assemble the necessary resources. Again, goods pass constantly from hand to hand in the course of marriage settlements, gifts to visitors, and a thousand other matters. By following any article through such social transactions and by asking the questions "What does this do? What does it mean to the people?" one can quickly learn a great deal about the local ways of living.

THE ISLAND FOODS

The islanders fall into several distinct types in terms of their economic base. In most parts of Malaysia, rice and fish are the principal or "staple" products. Along with rice, or even largely replacing it in the case of poorer people, may be corn, sweet potatoes, cassava (manioc or tapioca), beans, and other crops. These foods correspond to the wheat, potatoes, and beef of western diet.

East of the Molucca-Timor region of the Indies, rice production disappears except as it may have been introduced a little in modern days. Nearly all the South Sea peoples grow tropical roots and tubers for their vegetable staples, notably yams, taro, which is the root of a kind of lily, and sweet potatoes. They are also likely to depend more fully upon tropical fruits, such as the coconut, banana, and breadfruit, to round out the diet.

In swampy regions, notably on Borneo and New Guinea, sago may be a staple food. Sago is extracted from the pithy trunk of the mature sago palm at the time it begins to flower. Usually the palms grow wild, but sometimes they may be cultivated. Some peoples in New Guinea depend so much upon sago flour that they do little or no agriculture. On dry and barren atolls such as those of the Gilberts, a flour made from the seeds of the pandanus tree may be a staple food. Some atoll dwellers also grow coarse types of taro capable of surviving the high salt content of the water seeping into the pits in which they are cultivated. Nomadic forest peoples such as the Negritos of the Philippines gather a variety of wild vegetable products including roots, leaves, and fruits, as well as hunt small game for their food.

Two distinct kinds of rice cultivation exist—wet or paddy (sawah) rice, and dry or upland rice. The wet rice is produced in the flooded fields of the lowlands, or in step-like terraces which some peoples build on the mountainsides. Crude plows, pulled by water-buffaloes or cattle, are generally used to work up the soil, and the rice seedlings are grown in seed beds and then transplanted. "Dry" rice is grown without irrigation in rainy places, usually on the hills, and has a much scantier yield. The main agricultural tool needed is a sharp pointed "digging stick." This is also the standard gardening tool of the Oceanic peoples. Taro is similarly a wet or dry land crop. Each product, in fact, has its own growing conditions, and one can take it that the native knows about all that can be known about its cultivation, short of modern laboratory studies.

Where towns and fair-sized villages exist, it may be expected that the people are settled cultivators. This would be so, for example, in most lowland areas of Malaysia, and in the smaller Oceanic islands. The people may have been using the same fields for generations, perhaps even producing two major crops a year from them by painstaking methods of irrigation, using fertilizers, and otherwise working up the soil. Men, women, and children may be seen in the fields from early till late at important times in the cycle from planting to harvesting.

In the forested uplands of the larger islands, however, most cultivation is of a less intensive shifting type in which every season or so the people cut and burn a new clearing. From the native point of view, this is an easy method of cropping. The burning off of a new area fertilizes the soil with ash, and one crop or more can be taken off the land with maximum growing conditions. The people can then move on, only to return many years later, if at all, to plant another crop there. Groups practicing this type of cultivation are always small in numbers proportionate to the area, and they are more or less nomadic. If they have a base village, they are likely to be away from it much of the year, living in temporary shelters by their fields.

This latter type of cropping, often known under its general Malay name of *ladang* cultivation, is sometimes called "predatory" agriculture, because of the destruction it brings to the forests, and the uneconomic method of using the soil. In all countries of southeast Asia and Melanesia it is giving concern to governments because the valuable primary forest is never replaced directly when cut down. Instead, the clearings become choked with useless jungle thickets or speargrass, or else the hill slopes are bared by erosion. Efforts to get these peoples to settle down have so far rarely been successful. Previous to the war, some government authorities were trying to get the natives to replant their clearings with commercially valuable trees such as rubber or teak before they moved on.

Native communities almost invariably have some domestic livestock. The dog, the pig, and the chicken were carried by the islanders in their early migrations, even into Polynesia, though not every island there had all three of these animals when whites arrived. The Malaysians also had water-buffaloes and cattle. Horses, goats, sheep, ducks, and other livestock were probably brought in later. The Lesser Sunda Islands have long been famous for their breeds of ponies, grazed on parklike grasslands there which are produced by the dry monsoon winds blowing into this region annually from Australia.

Pigs and chickens may provide the main sanitary service of a native village. Mohammedans, however, have a taboo against pigs, and so do not keep them around. Chicken is the most likely food a visitor will be served in a native village. Water-buffaloes and cattle are used as draft animals, and a common sight in places like the Philippines is to see a small child perched on a water-buffalo taking it to its favorite mud pool to cool off. It is wise for a stranger not to come too close to this animal, especially if it is encountered roving loose. He may have to stay perched up a tree for quite a while.

Fish is the staple flesh diet of nearly all the island peoples other than those few living away from the coast and inland waterways, and most islanders prefer fish to any other flesh food. They eat it not only fresh and sometimes raw, but also dried, smoked, salted, and perhaps pickled. The visitor will note the attention given to canoes and fishing gear, and will undoubtedly learn a great deal from native fishing methods. Some peoples cultivate fish in artificial ponds, with either salt or fresh water. They may even collect small fish, together with crabs, snails, and other aquatic foods, from rice or taro beds when these are flooded for irrigation purposes.

The forest and sea provide a very wide range of other products. Some peoples in the outer areas hunt extensively for wild hog, deer, birds, edible reptiles, and other animals. They may burn off grasslands in great annual drives. Generally speaking, however, game is scarce near native settlements because of continuous hunting through the generations. Plants of the forest and edible seaweeds may also be part of the regular food supply.

Too much cannot be said about watching the natives or getting their advice about the use of local resources. Apart from their regular foods they know of numerous kinds of emergency foods in their localities, such as the leaves, stalks, flowers, fruits, and roots of land and water plants that may yield food and drink, and edible animals such as birds, reptiles, and insects. They know what is poisonous, and may turn poisons to use, as with the derris root and barringtonia nut, employed as fish poisons but not harmful to man. They can also tell about the qualities of local timbers, pointing out for example those least vulnerable to insects, or those making the best firewood. They know what local fibers are best used for emergency cord and rope. They can gather leaves and fruit of medicinal value, capable of being used like the herbal drugs of western drugstores; their healers generally employ such treatments along with their magic mumbo-jumbo or primitive psychotherapy.

Certain plants and animals are of particular usefulness to the islanders because of the wide range of products they supply. Number one on the list in many areas is the coconut palm. An amazing array of dishes and liquids can be obtained from the coconut fruit at various stages of growth, including even the equivalent of cream (squeezed from the grated white flesh) and cheese (the lump in a sprouting fallen nut). The tree also provides syrup or sugar, cloth, plaiting materials, fiber from the husk, and other products. The atoll dwellers, who have such a limited range of plants, make fullest use of the coconut. An example of an animal that is similarly useful is the cassowary bird of New Guinea, which provides flesh food, sinews, bones for weapons, feathers for decoration, and other materials. The newcomer's own curiosity will lead him to find other all-in-one resources of this kind in any place to which he goes.

SURPLUSES

Native communities can nearly always supply small amounts of foodstuffs to visitors. Ordinarily, however, they do not have any large food surpluses, and a force of even a few dozen soldiers or a small civilian party might quickly eat out their gardens and livestock.

The most likely time to get native foods in any large quantity is just after the harvesting of seasonal crops, if any. In the New Guinea region, for example, the yam crop usually ripens at about the end of the wet season and the same is true of the main rice harvest in the Malaysian islands. But if such foods are taken over in large amounts, there is a strong chance that the people may have to be helped later to carry over the lean period before the next harvest. It may be wiser to try to stimulate native output of foods that do not cut so much into the regular larder, for example, making more sago flour in some districts, or doing extra fishing along the coasts. Even here, one will need to watch that the normal balance of supply is not upset to a point where later scarcities are created.

An important reason why the native peoples do not lay up large stocks is the problem of storage. Many foodstuffs deteriorate rapidly in these tropical, insect-ridden areas, where ice has perhaps never been heard of. The natives therefore adopt a method of living storage by which they gather perishable foods from their gardens and other sources just before such supplies are needed. Those products which can be kept, such as rice, tubers, sago flour, and preserved fish, may be kept in special insect-proof storehouses, or in pits or jars.

The wisest approach in trying to get supplies at a native settlement is to go to the headman or chief. He will be able to direct the people in whatever extra effort is needed, while his household is the one most likely to have large accumulations of stored foods.

National Museum and Press Assn.

Plate 15

Upper. "Stone money" of Yap is wealth. Cut from reef rock in the Palau Islands, some "coins" are 12 feet in diameter. Here they stand against a ceremonial platform of the village council house.

Lower. The market in Papeete, French Oceania, is thronged with shoppers buying seafoods of many kinds and other native edibles.

Pan Pacific Press and U.S. Marine

PLATE 16

Upper. Lei sellers in Honolulu. Natives living in the cities and ports are often able to make a living by selling native craftwork.

Lower left. How islanders shred the flesh of a coconut to make coconut cream or pudding. The chisel-like blade may be of wood or tortoise shell.

Lower right. A Samoan youth deftly plaits a basket from a coconut palm leaf split down the middle, to carry coconuts which he has husked. He wears a colorful red and white *lavalava* or waistcloth.

TRADE AND MONEY

A few native communities in remoter areas were wholly self-sufficient before the white man came. They produced everything they required, and at most the local types of wealth were passed back and forth among kinsmen and neighbors within their settlements. But the great number of natives carried on at least minor bartering and trading to round out their needs.

Many of these traditional forms of trade are still being carried on today. The visitor may see natives going on foot or by canoe for their periodic trading "walkabout." One of the most usual exchange relations is between peoples who live along the coasts or on small offshore islands, and those living in the interior. The former supply marine products, including fish, salt, shell, and manufactured shell-money. In return the latter may give garden and forest products such as vegetables, lumber, rattan, and wild honey. Here and there a lucky group controls some special resource, as for example good clay for pot-making, metal ore deposits, or an interior salt spring, and so their territory serves as a miniature industrial center for surrounding peoples. Or a group may have a corner on some special skill like making a particular pattern of mat, or manufacturing especially seaworthy canoes.

Native articles are often passed from group to group along established trade routes for long distances, sometimes in New Guinea and Borneo for hundreds of miles. Before white governments stopped native warfare, even peoples who ordinarily used to kill one another at sight might have special truce arrangements through which they could exchange articles. A few groups have concentrated on the role of middlemen, carrying goods back and forth along the coast or the big rivers, as with the Buginese of the southern Celebes and the Schouten Islanders and Dobuans of north New Guinea. Some places, such as the little town of Dobo in the Aru Islands, are famed as marketing centers to which natives may come from far and wide.

Native trading may consist of straight buying and selling, or it may be more subtly and ceremoniously carried on by gift exchanges, much as the white man gives Christmas and birthday presents. In the Oceanic islands passing of goods has been almost wholly of the latter type, and no common denominator of money was used. Even so-called "shell-money" is hardly money in the commercial sense, but rather a form of ceremonial wealth which was passed from hand to hand and accumulated to serve social rather than economic ends. By native custom a person who is given a "gift" is expected to return in due course something of equivalent value to the giver. Instead of using a bank, the native remembers his debits and credits in terms of such reciprocal giving.

Natives frequently pass over such "gifts" to the newcomer in ceremonious fashion, usually not asking for anything in return. It is from this custom that the tradition has grown up of the "generosity" of the South Sea islanders. But if the recipient wants to be thought well of, and not privately criticized as an ingrate, he should take the first opportunity to return something about equivalent in money or goods. He will then have settled what would otherwise be an outstanding social account. At the same time a visitor should be careful about passing out too much in the way of gifts, or "raising the ante" too much on native gifts, as this puts the native under an obligation which, if he is an honest person, he may find difficulty in matching reciprocally.

Such gift exchanges, without any use of money, are also found as a normal part of life in Malaysian communities. But large areas of Malaysia have long been touched, in addition, by commercial trading. The early Indian, Arab, and Chinese merchants brought to places such as Sumatra and the "Spice

Islands" (Moluccas) their own keen traditions of commerce and finance. Later, throughout the Pacific, white and Chinese traders introduced group after group to modern ideas of business.

It is a striking fact, however, that even yet very few natives anywhere in these countries have taken up storekeeping or other modern commercial occupations. Even in well-developed places such as the Philippines, merchandising and banking are almost wholly in the hands of the whites, Chinese, Arabs, and other non-native groups. In some places, indeed, any native who attempted to open a store might well have all his goods appropriated by relatives, with at most a polite thanks, under the share-and-share philosophy. At most, natives are likely to carry on trading and hawking on a minor scale around the town centers, especially in Malaysia. Often it is the wife in a household who supplements the regular source of livelihood with a little business outside the house or at the community marketplace. Even where the people now have crop surpluses, or other products for sale, these are nearly always disposed of to a non-native middleman who handles the outside marketing—and takes large profits. In a few places a beginning is being made with cooperative marketing by native communities. In the Gilbert Islands the one commercial resource, copra, has been handled successfully during recent years through native cooperatives.

Granting this lack of participation in business pursuits, native peoples in all but the remotest districts have become quite used to going to the store or market to meet certain of their needs. As indicated already, some manufactured goods from the outside world have by now become essentials to them, supplementing the articles they make for themselves at home. An inventory of any native trading store in the islands is likely to show much the same goods, among them metal tools such as knives, razor-blades, and fish-hooks, cloth and cloth goods, combs and umbrellas, and perhaps bicycles. Some of these articles are regarded as necessities; others are luxuries that the people buy for show and pleasure. Imported foods such as canned meat are generally in the latter class, except around the towns where people have to depend more or less wholly on store foods.

In the Japanese-occupied areas, the natives have been feeling the pinch of acute shortage in most of these trade goods. In fact, many districts have been short of them for years, because of the depression of the thirties and the dislocation of trade after 1939 when Britain, Holland, and France entered the war. The Japanese have rarely been able to supply trade articles in any quantity, if at all. The natives will be looking forward just as keenly as the white man does to getting the war over with, and things back to normal. The relations of the Japanese with the islanders have not been helped by their introduction of paper money, something to which most natives have never been accustomed. Before the war, they nearly always handled money in the form of substantial silver coins.

Native communities, even in remote districts, have developed needs for money at least in small amounts. In addition to purchasing goods at the trading store, they usually have to pay to the government an annual head tax for every adult male. In some places the government also collects taxes on dogs, and makes small charges for medical and other services, while natives who get into trouble may have to pay fines. Then, too, there may be church collections, usually in the form of one large annual gift. Money may also be needed to pay landlords and moneylenders. Payments of all these kinds may be met in goods, such as crops, or in services, such as working on the roads in the case of government dues. But increasingly they involve the direct handling of money.

A native needing money is likely to go first to his relatives to see whether he can get it under the traditional give-and-take system. Failing this, he usually has two alternatives. One is to sell his labor or that of a member of his family, usually a young man, by finding a wage-earning job. If there is no casual work to be found in the district, he or his substitute may have to go to one of the port centers, or sign up as a contract laborer to work at some plantation or mine. Incidentally, governments have found that taxes are a great stimulus to getting natives to work as laborers. Or the native in need of money may sell some commodity which is in demand for commerce, either cultivated crops, or craftwork, or natural products of forest and ocean.

The native who grows crops for sale rarely goes beyond the few products which require merely a small part of his land and a minimum of labor, care, and technical skill. He is, of course, virtually ruled out from growing products which require large capital investment or elaborate processing, and usually from producing those calling for very uniform standards of quality. The most widely produced native commodity is the dried flesh of the coconut, copra, which yields vegetable oil. The men may be seen deftly extracting the white flesh from the nuts with their knives, and women and children drying it in the sun. This is the standard native product of the South Seas, and is collected by copra schooners and cutters from all the little bays and islands for trans-shipment at the central ports. One has to get used to its pungent oily odor.

In Malaysia, natives may also sell rice, cassava (tapioca), coffee, spices such as pepper, kapok, and several other crops. An increasing number, especially in Sumatra and Borneo, even plant hevea (rubber) trees which they tap when needs arise. With hundreds of thousands of families adding their small quotas of such products, the native export crops added up before the war to quite impressive figures.

Native communities living in or near the forests may also gather forest products. Some collect gums and resins, such as jelutong, which is a base for chewing-gum, and copal or dammar, used in paints and varnishes. Rattan for making furniture, mangrove bark from which tanning extract is obtained, sago, and beeswax are among other products of the forest. Formerly the New Guinea area had a rich trade in the feathered skins of the bird-of-paradise, but governments now prohibit killing of these rare birds.

Peoples who live by the sea may collect commercially valuable kinds of shell, including mother-of-pearl, trochus, and tortoise-shell. They may also sell dried sea-slugs (bêche-de-mer or trepang) which go to China, fancy coral, and perhaps pearls. But pearl diving, once a thriving activity, is now largely a thing of the past because of over-exploitation, lack of markets, and the production of artificial and cultivated pearls. It is carried on nowadays mainly in the Aru and Torres Straits Islands north of Australia and in the Trobriand Islands off eastern New Guinea. In some parts of Malaysia and New Guinea the natives do a little mining of gold and silver, but nearly all mineral exploitation is in the hands of non-natives.

If natives are being paid in money for goods or services, the best rule is to keep to whatever levels of payment are locally current. Rates are nearly always fixed by the government for standard services, and it is unwise to overpay or tip, for then the natives are likely to think that the person concerned is easy prey and they will try to beat him at every chance. The whole economy of a district can be thrown out of gear by visitors flinging their money around carelessly, for example in getting natives to climb coconut trees, to do laundry, or to rent bicycles. A soldier or civilian should remember that by local standards his pay makes him fabulously rich, and the natives are practically sure to resent any ostentatious display of superior wealth.

TENANCY AND USURY

In the Oceanic islands, native households or individuals nearly always control their own houses and gardens as small independent holders. They may give some customary "tribute" or share of produce to a chief or clan elder within whose sphere of authority they lie, but there is rarely anything equivalent to a landlord-tenant relation. In Malaysia, by contrast, tenancy is very widespread, especially in the crowded riceland areas. A considerable part of the population is eking out the barest subsistence as tenants or sharecroppers, caught as were their parents before them in bondage and indebtedness to landlords, with little chance of extricating themselves. Along with tenancy, the typical Oriental custom of usury is widespread. Interest in this part of the world may run anywhere up to several hundred per cent per annum.

As may be expected, tenancy and usury are the most serious economic problems for the native in the Malaysian area. They are back of the serious agrarian unrest which has broken out from time to time. The situation is perhaps worse in the Philippines than anywhere else. The 1939 census of the Commonwealth showed that only about forty per cent of Filipino families own their house and land, and of the rest, seventeen per cent own neither their house nor their land. Juan de la Cruz, the "John Doe" of the Philippines, is typically a tenant farmer, working a tiny holding, and in constant debt to his landlord. The bulk of the good agricultural land is owned by a landlord or squire class called the *caciques*, somewhat like the grandees of Spain.

Some of these landlords show close personal interest in their tenants, much as did the chiefs of former times from whom many are descended. But the tendency is for them to settle in the cities and leave the handling of their affairs to agents. As population increases and the remaining small independent holdings are divided up among many children, more and more of the people have to go into debt and mortgage their land to keep body and soul together, which means that tenancy is noticeably on the increase. The tenant may even have to sell his meager share of the rice crop, and buy foods that are inferior for his family.

The small Malaysian rice farmer is most likely to be caught short in the months before his new crop comes to harvest. If his relatives cannot help him, he may try to tide himself over by taking some of his household property to a local pawnshop, from which he can redeem it later. Or he may be forced to go to a rich man in the community, usually a landlord, or to a professional moneylender. The pawnbroker or moneylender is nearly always a Chinese, an Indian, or an Arab. The "instalment Chinese" is an especially familiar sight in the villages, where he collects his few coins of interest or principal. According to western standards, these money transactions are usually insignificant in amount, but to the local people they represent high finance.

Governments have tried to meet these problems in various ways. In Java, for example, the authorities established government pawnshops, small village banks from which needy persons can get money or grain, and other supervised sources of credit. They have also encouraged the development of native cooperatives, and tried to limit the legal rates of interest. Other governments in Malaysia have taken steps along the same general lines. But the fundamental problems of tenancy and usury still remain little touched. It has been difficult to get measures passed by local legislatures to better the lot of tenants. Such practices are rooted in the local customary law of these regions, and any proposed change meets with strong opposition from influential groups. In the less crowded outer districts, the problems are of course less serious.

POPULATION PRESSURE AND RESETTLEMENT

Some parts of the islands are by now faced with a growing problem of population pressure. Often the region immediately around a town or plantation area is overcrowded because part of the land has been sold or leased to outsiders, and the natives who flock in to these places also try to get land so as to maintain themselves. Some of the tiny islands, too, with limited resources, are now getting seriously overpopulated. Modern health measures are cutting down the death-rate, and the local people are increasing rapidly in numbers. For years, people from certain small islands like the Tokelaus and Ellices have been moving out to the ports in the larger islands to try to get a living. Before the war, the British government transferred about two thousand Gilbert Islanders from their crowded atoll homes to new settlements in the Phoenix Islands.

The most serious instance of crowding, however, is in the island of Java. In recent years, the Indies government has assisted thousands of Javanese families to move to southern Sumatra and other places. Yet always more mouths come along to fill in the home villages. As little new land can be broken in to cultivation on Java, the authorities have been encouraging the growth of small home industries as a means of supplementing the people's income. In the northern Philippines, too, hundreds of thousands of Ilocanos from the crowded Ilocos coast north of Manila have been pioneering new homes, with or without government assistance, many coming even to Hawaii and the United States. In the southern Philippines, Visayans from densely populated Cebu have been spilling over into Mindanao and other relatively empty islands.

The island peoples have deep attachments to their ancestral homes. Only the most needy families, therefore, are likely to migrate permanently in this way. But many of the poorest people cannot move, not only because they have no resources to stake their venture, but also because they are in debt to landlords who will not release them. They would be sent to prison if they tried to leave. This helps to explain the apparent paradox that so much land in Malaysia still remains little populated, while other areas are crowded. Before the war the governments were trying to step up the rate of resettlement by opening up land and giving financial aid, but so far their schemes have been small compared to the magnitude of the problem.

EATING HABITS

It is difficult to measure the diet of the island peoples, because their eating habits are often very different from those of the white man. Instead of having three meals more or less regularly each day, they may have two, or possibly only one large one. Or they may snack much more often, or else eat quite irregularly. They may live on little food for a period, then gorge themselves when some ceremony brings a feast. One becomes amazed at the variations to which the human digestive system can be trained.

The same is true of what the islanders eat. In addition to staple foods such as have been referred to already, they may add all kinds of titbits to their diet, including wild game, insects, grubs, eggs of birds and reptiles, small snails, leaves and fruits from the forest, seaweeds, fungus growths, and much else. It would be hard to keep track of the whole range of food supply. In Java, certain foods like soybeans and peanuts are allowed to accumulate moulds before being eaten, and it is interesting to note that scientific analysis has shown these to be mainly produced by the micro-organisms from which the drug penicillin comes. Throughout Malaysia, the people use large amounts of spice in their foods, especially pepper. Sometimes foods are allowed to ferment or rot before being eaten, and unless a person enjoys limburger he may want to keep well to windward.

Enough is now known of native foods to indicate that they can supply an adequate diet. Even without milk, butter, and other staples which Westerners use, the native peoples may have good teeth and hardy bodies. This is particularly true of the many groups who produce their own foods locally in the traditional ways. Here and there such native-style diets may not be too adequate, as perhaps with some of the sago-eating peoples of Melanesia whose food appears to lean heavily to the side of starch. But the really serious problems of nutrition are found among the poorer classes on the crowded ricelands, where food supply is cut to the minimum. They also occur in the towns and labor barracks where the people depend mostly upon imported foods. The use of white polished rice, instead of the unpolished rice eaten in the rural districts where the grain is husked at home, is the worst feature of modern diet, as it leads to beriberi and other deficiency diseases. Canned foods, too, are poor substitutes for the fresh products, especially as they are often of low quality. Generally speaking, the bad teeth of natives in the crowded areas and towns give visible evidence of poor and unbalanced diets.

Food to the native is far more than something that keeps a person alive. Just as in western communities, it serves all sorts of social ends connected with entertainment, display, and even religious ritual. The newcomer will soon learn in any place to distinguish the ordinary daily foods from what might be called "feast foods." The natives have their special drinks and dishes, like turkey or birthday cake, which they reserve for festivals, and perhaps for religious sacrifices. In many areas, for example, pigs are killed and eaten only on such occasions, and the meat may be carved and distributed with elaborate ceremony.

For extra special celebrations native foods may be piled mountains high. Guests as well as local people may be required by custom to bring along their quotas. Plentiful opportunity is usually given for everyone to admire the display, and to note who contributed what, before the feast proceeds. Any important personage such as a rajah or chief is likely to have to put on showy spreads from time to time if he wishes to keep his prestige. The same is true of Ambassador So-and-so, or Mrs. Such-and-such, in high circles back home.

DRINKS AND NARCOTICS

In the rice regions, the people generally make rice wine or beer. These brews are likely to be very heady, especially the thick dregs at the bottom of a jar. They are often drunk with high ceremony. Sugarcane wine may be favored instead, or some other fermented drink such as toddy from the flower spathes of certain palm trees, including the coconut and nipa, or the juices of various tropical fruits. Many natives have become great drinkers of coffee or tea. By contrast, some may never drink anything but water and perhaps coconut juice.

In parts of Polynesia and eastern Melanesia, a narcotic drink is made from a peppery root best known under the name *kava*. Sometimes drinking it is made an essential part of all ceremony and entertainment, and kava may be brewed and drunk with elaborate dramatics, notably in Fiji and Samoa. Old-timers among the white residents often become just as addicted to kava as the natives, even though the first reaction of a visitor is usually one of dislike for the peppery, astringent taste.

In many parts of the southwest Pacific, the natives chew "betel." A slice of the betel or areca nut is wrapped along with some lime in a pepper leaf to make a quid. When chewed, it produces a bright red juice which addicts usually spit around so that the place looks like a battlefield. It has a narcotic effect and also blackens the teeth. Some peoples have the custom of

LIVELIHOOD 77

giving betel to one another when they meet, as a sign of courtesy and friendliness.

Nearly all natives today are great smokers, even perhaps down to small children. Tobacco may be grown in native gardens, in which case one will probably find it impossibly rank. But most tobacco is imported, frequently in the form of black ropelike "twist" or sticks. In Melanesia, special American tobacco (usually black Emu, twenty-six sticks to the pound) is used widely as a secondary currency to pay for native goods and services. Natives will accept politely the western brands of cigarettes, but they may not get much "kick" out of them. In some districts stick tobacco will get things done that money cannot.

COOKING AND FIRE-MAKING

Native cooking methods are worth watching, and some of them worth learning. Many Oceanic peoples use a pit or underground oven to steam their foods, first heating stones in a fire within the pit, and then putting the food in leaves on top of the stones and covering the whole with earth. In communities which use pottery, a fireplace may be made with three or more stones for the cooking pot to rest on. Water may be boiled in a coconut shell or a bamboo tube by dropping in hot stones. Fish may be baked in a fire after coating them with clay. Natives may soften tough meat by wrapping it for an hour in papaya leaves. These are just a few of the many ideas to be gained from native skills.

Natives may still be able to produce fire by rubbing or spinning one stick in the groove of another, or in some other traditional way. Most of them, however, have long since abandoned such laborious methods in favor of matches. A white man will probably never succeed in getting a light by native methods, so the wise thing is for him to take along an emergency supply of matches in waterproof wrapping, and if possible a burning glass, on any special expedition. Natives often bury a smouldering log such as a piece of coconut trunk if they are coming back to the same camp, or carry this along with them to their next camp. Before the war, kerosene lamps and even sometimes electricity were replacing the older fires or oil flares to give light in native houses. These were all the more appreciated because many native groups have the custom of keeping lights in their houses at night to ward off spirits and ghosts. Such peoples have not been enjoying blackout regulations.

NATIVE HANDICRAFTS AND INDUSTRIES

The islanders, used to working directly with the raw materials of nature, are nearly always skilful with their hands. Their crafts and industries are worth close examination, both for their own interest and because the products and the craftsmen themselves may often prove useful. Even the newcomer may quickly learn to copy some of the native handiwork, as for example a simple criss-cross plaiting which can provide him speedily with baskets, bedding, and other handy articles, or a method of knotting with which a fishnet can be made from cord.

Each people met with will have its own traditional types of handicraft, depending on its needs and tastes for utensils, furnishings, ornaments, musical instruments, and other material goods. Just as a mail-order catalog is a record of the gear which the white man's civilization favors, so one can make an inventory of what the native accumulates. Sometimes it does not add up to much. A band of forest Negritos is interested only in the few essential tools and other objects it can carry along in its wanderings. But usually such equipment is fairly elaborate.

Nearly always any group lavishes special effort on certain crafts, turning them into arts. Among South Sea Islanders, some groups concentrate major attention on woodwork, producing such works of art as the grotesque carvings of the New Zealand Maori and the carved and inlaid food-bowls of the Solomons. Others put their best efforts into weaving or plaiting, metal work, making bone, shell or feather ornaments, or even stone carving. These focal points of craft work give important clues for understanding local ideas and beliefs. Nearly always they are linked closely with religious matters and surrounded with ritual.

Perhaps the best-known native handwork in the area is the making of *batik* cloth in Java. The batik designs are prepared by putting wax on the parts not to be tinted, then boiling it off after the dyes have been applied. In western areas of the Pacific, various types of looms are used to weave loincloths, skirts, blankets, grave wrappings, and other articles, though nowadays imported thread or yarn usually replaces the local kind of fiber. Farther east in the Pacific, weaving is replaced by plaiting, in which the strands of coconut leaf, pandanus leaf, or other material are criss-crossed, without one set of elements being warped tight on a loom. In some places barkcloth (tapa) is still beaten out from the paper-mulberry and other barks to make headbands, waistcloths, or bedding.

Metalworking is an important industry in Malaysia. For many centuries, iron, copper, gold, and silver have been traded from certain mining centers, the first two usually in the form of bars and wire. Native smiths have then shaped the metals into the favored local styles of knives, axes, earrings, and other objects, producing excellent work in spite of the crudeness of their little forges. In the larger centers, skilled craftsmen have made jewelry and other special wares, bringing together the elaborate metalworking traditions of both the Indian and the Mohammedan Arab civilizations. In Oceania, where metal ores have rarely been accessible, the people have developed their traditional crafts with the materials available to them, such as stone, bone, shell, wood, fibers, and feathers. The small islands east and north of Fiji have not even had clay to make pottery ware as do many peoples in the western Pacific.

In modern times, many native industries have been yielding ground with the coming of the trade store and machine-made goods. As regards textiles, for example, the islanders are following along the same lines as the western peoples did several generations ago in giving up home spinning. Some crafts have gone out of existence altogether, except in remote areas, as with making stone adzes.

Nevertheless several influences are keeping native crafts alive. For one thing, such peoples often continue to use their traditional native articles, such as barkcloth or mat garments, on ceremonial occasions, even though they go to the trade store for every-day needs. Or such articles may be of some conservatively held design, or meet some special local need, as with a type of fishnet, or a pestle and mortar for husking rice. Some new commercial stimulus like the tourist trade may keep craftsmen at work making articles of traditional pattern. With the shortages created by the Japanese invasion, many groups will have had to go back more or less to their older industries, just as some did during the depression of the early thirties.

Native craftsmen have usually been quite ready to take over from the white man whatever tools and techniques they think will be of use to them. Islanders may cut designs on their canoe paddles with a hammer and chisel. They also make articles of modern design, if a market can be found for them. In some centers, profitable industries have developed such as plaiting of hats, embroidering, or carving objects for the tourist trade. The aptitude of natives with their hands has also enabled them to get employment as mechanics, radio operators, motor drivers, engineers, and crewmen on the small craft of the islands, and as factory workers in the urban centers. This pool of skilled native workers may be of great help if tapped for military or or other purposes.

San Francisco Chronicle Library and Netherlands Information Bureau

PLATE 17

Upper. Outside a Manila church, vendors sell candles, religious books, and other sacred objects. Sometimes fairs are held in the church grounds.
Lower. Javanese women add to the family income by working in textile mills and in other industries. They wear typical jacket (*badjou*) and skirt (*kain*).

Pan Pacific

PLATE 18

Upper. The underground oven: a pig and other foods have been placed on the hot stones and are about to be covered with leaves, mats and then a top layer of earth. Hot stones are put inside the pig.

Lower. The South Seas has its cowboys. A colorful *paniola,* or cowhand, of one of the great ranches in Hawaii. Many islanders have taken keenly to horseback riding since these animals have been brought in.

WORK, CONTRACT LABOR

Contrary to much popular opinion, native peoples in the tropics obviously do not get their food and other necessaries without real effort. The myth of the lazy native has come either from superficial observation of native work habits or from the fact that many native groups have not been interested in working as laborers in the white man's service.

The truth is that, given the right incentives, such peoples will work hard and well, particularly if the tasks and the timetable are fitted to their traditional habits and ideas. The visitor has only to watch a native family at work in its garden, or a co-operative working-bee constructing a house to realize this. By taking note of the work calendar of natives over a period, or of the way a carrier boy handles a load or a native crew paddles or rows a boat, it will be seen that these people put keen effort into any job they consider worthwhile or necessary—and amazing prodigies of energy if the occasion is crucial enough.

Yet their habits of working, their organization and timing of a job, and that more elusive thing, their philosophy of work, are likely to be very different from those of the white man—customs that are tied in with regular employment on some specialized job, with calendars and factory whistles, and with the austere Biblical directive: "In the sweat of thy face shalt thou eat bread." Labor in these native communities does not consist of continuous effort on the same task. Instead, it is highly varied, and is governed by the broken rhythms of seasonal and weather changes, and by the sudden emergencies that life close to nature presents.

When work has to be done, it is usually carried out by groups rather than by individuals. Its drudgery aspects are relieved by rhythmic activity, chanting, story-telling, joking, gossiping, and other accompaniments which make it as far as possible an enjoyable social activity. If major tasks have to be performed, such as planting or harvesting a crop, or going on an important fishing or trading expedition, the activity is usually preceded, interspersed, and followed up with festivals and ceremonies which rally the group morale and step up energies to the required tension for carrying the work through. Such occasions are also stamped with the solemnities of religious belief and ritual which underscore the importance of the work, and rally supernatural forces to aid in the effort. Through doing tasks well, or by showing greater skill than his fellows, the individual wins the approval and admiration of his group, and so enhances his social status. The slacker is a *rara avis* under such a system.

To get natives to work, therefore, apart from using a bayonet point in the Japanese manner, calls for as much knowledge as possible of their local work customs. The energy is there; the problem is to harness it by way of the right incentives and methods of organization. The ordinary native, as an individual, may show little enthusiasm for work of the kind you may want done, unless he happens to have some special need that will compensate him for leaving his village and neglecting his own more or less busy concerns. Obviously, therefore, it is best to go to the traditional directors or controllers of the community labor supply, usually the headmen, chiefs, or clan elders. If the task permits, any familiar working-bee methods may be used to advantage, and singing and noisy chatter tolerated in the interests of getting the work done. Some peoples will prefer to be supervised closely and to receive plenty of advice, but others will resent this. Orders and comments should be given only to their equivalent of a foreman.

When necessary, it should be possible to step up the pace of a task by finding the right incentives. Special gifts and bonuses may accomplish this, given, of course, to any responsible leaders as well as to the actual workers. If social or religious pressures can be rallied to back up the work, so much the better. Some special recognition given to each phase of the work as it is rounded off will usually help, as also at the completion of the task, especially if these ceremonious occasions involve some extra "feast-food." Anyone handling native workers must always be prepared to have them suddenly quit, and then it is up to him to discover why. Perhaps a taboo was broken, or a religious holiday is being observed, or some crisis exists in their home communities.

Rightly handled, native workers will usually be found teachable, responsible, and loyal. As to payment, the various government authorities have long had fixed pay scales for labor of various kinds, as indicated already, and it is best to conform to the familiar pattern. Payment may be made, according to local usage and preference, in money or in stick tobacco or other trade articles. The great shortage of consumer goods brought about by the war should make the task of getting native workers much easier in many districts than it was in peace-time.

As already indicated, most Pacific island areas have had systems of contract labor. In earlier days many thousands of natives were recruited or kidnapped through the notorious "blackbirding" system, often never getting back to their homes. Memories of this still linger, especially in Melanesian islands. In recent decades, however, the governments have kept close control over labor recruiting and conditions of employment, though they still frequently allow the indenture system by which the laborer can be imprisoned if he tries to leave his employer or otherwise breaks the contract which he signs.

Labor recruiting has usually been done by licensed recruiters, who get a certain sum for each native signed on. In Australian New Guinea, the Solomons and New Hebrides and the Gilberts, serving as a contract laborer has become almost a regular part of the career of a young man. In Malaysia the great labor pools have been the crowded areas of Java, Tonkin (Indochina), the northern and central Philippines, and of course China and India. "Free" labor is increasingly used in the islands, that is, without indenture, especially for work near the homes of the natives and for shorter periods.

PROPERTY

Whenever a person wants to buy, rent, or borrow articles from natives, or to get the use of their land or other property, he will uncover local customs and ideas regarding ownership which are often strangely different from those of western countries. Each people has its own exact property rules defined by its "customary law," and as in white society, these form one of the main concerns of law and order.

It is an error to think that so-called primitives, in the islands or elsewhere, share all their goods communally or collectively. Some kinds of property they do share, just as there is public ownership of certain land and goods in any western country. Frequently the ocean offshore, together with any reefs and lagoon and also the forests back of a settlement, are held in this way, as well as any public buildings and other community property within the settlement itself. Here, as in the West, the local rules define the rights and duties of everyone regarding their use, and provide whatever safeguards are necessary to preserve them in good condition.

Other kinds of property may be held by individuals or by groups of individuals such as clans, kin groups, or households. Just what is involved in such possession, however, is frequently complex, so that one may get tangled and tripped. Even when a fruit tree or a fishnet appears to be owned by a particular individual or family, there may be other individuals or families who exercise some authority over it—as, for example, a superior chief or a senior family line—or relatives and fellow villagers who have traditional rights of using it. One of the most serious causes of trouble between white settlers and the native peoples along Pacific frontiers came from the fact that the whites bought land from its "owners" in the orthodox manner of a western property transaction, only to find that all they had bought were the rights of the individuals concerned, so that the vested interests of perhaps numerous other persons came to light once the settler tried to occupy and fence off the property.

Perhaps the safest lead is to forget conventional terms and ideas relating to property, such as "owner" or "borrower" with their impersonal and commercial flavor, and instead, to ask as regards any piece of native property: "Who has rights, equities, interests in it?" "Who has duties and responsibilities toward it?" What will be found, perhaps, is that, under the customary law of the people concerned, more than one person has authority over the property, while others have rights of use under given conditions. The authority aspect is particularly linked with prestige, so that it usually pertains to persons of high social status such as heads of families, clan elders, chiefs, or rajahs. The use aspect is its every-day practical significance. Complex and shadowy as these rights, interests, and responsibilities often are, pyramiding up through the ranks of the society and spreading outward along lines of family and community cooperation, they can usually be run to earth, and the appropriate person or persons found who have the power of disposal, or who can arrange it.

Such intricate property arrangements are obviously not "communism" or "collectivism" in the vague sense that most people think of the terms, for all the constituent rights of individuals are carefully defined. It can be seen, however, how such customs, involving reciprocal give-and-take relations, form one of the main forces knitting these little social and community groups into a working whole. At the funeral of an important person, a visitor may get a good demonstration of the local property customs, because at such a time all the rights and duties of the deceased individual have to be disposed of by inheritance. He will probably see the equivalent of western lawyers, usually the elders who are experts in the customary law, managing the redistribution.

Nowadays such property arrangements usually extend to cover the possession of money and other modern-style wealth. This will account for something that may annoy the newcomer the first time he experiences it, namely a chief, family head, or even the local pastor appropriating much or all of the wages paid to a young man for the work he has done, or of the money given to a native family for services rendered.

THE ECONOMIC FUTURE

Native economic systems as sketched here have been the subject of much discussion and even controversy. In earlier days, governing authorities usually did their best to encourage the native peoples to produce crops for export, and to adopt western habits of work and individualistic property customs. Then came the depression period of the last decade, with glutted markets and low prices. Unsold products piled up in the villages, and unemployment became rife in the port and industrial centers. Policy shifted as a result toward encouraging native self-sufficiency, especially in foodstuffs, and toward keeping the native on his land.

The welfare of native communities depends on striking a balance as far as possible between these two policies. Such people cannot be kept at a purely subsistence level, nor will they remain entirely rural. They already have needs for goods which can be met only by way of the trade store, and their wants and ambitions are slowly but steadily increasing. Correspondingly, they must have opportunity for selling local products such as crops or craftwork, or for earning money in other ways. An increasing number of the educated youth will want to try themselves out in the more specialized occupations, including the professions. Yet overstimulation of native communities in commercial pursuits exposes them to the vagaries of world markets, and throws traditional customs seriously out of gear. Actually communities and individuals are adjusting at their own pace to modern economic opportunities, and it is equally disorganizing to push them too fast or to try to hold them back.

6. Home Conditions

THE ISLAND PEOPLES rarely live on scattered individual holdings, as American farmers do. Instead they cluster in settlements. This fundamental pattern of living gives them protection from enemies and from harmful spirits and ghosts. It also opens the way to many economic and social advantages which come from cooperating with kinsmen and neighbors.

Some native peoples traditionally favor small hamlets, usually of close relatives, and possibly having from three to twenty huts. Others have more substantial villages, with perhaps from 200 to 2,000 inhabitants. Towns larger than this are nearly always of modern growth, having developed under the influence of trade and commerce. A few centers, however, such as Malacca and Ternate, took form long before European merchants came into the area. In the Malay-speaking regions the native quarter of a town or city is called a *kampong*.

Settlements are most often located along the palm-fringed beaches or on the banks of inland waterways, where the people can draw upon aquatic resources and have easy means of travel and transport by water. A person becoming lost in the uplands has his best chance of finding natives, especially friendly natives, if he gets to the coast or to a river as soon as possible. In the trade-wind belt, settlements are usually thickest on the lee shore. Coastal peoples sometimes build their settlements actually out in the water on piles, or on sandbanks, reefs, or artificially made islets. This is usually because the shores are muddy or swampy, or because the people have wanted protection from enemies living inland. Peoples of the swamplands may also live a largely aquatic existence.

San Francisco Chronicle Library and Netherlands Information Bureau

PLATE 19

Upper. A city such as Manila shows the old and the new: an early Spanish church, modern buildings, and the combination of Western and traditional dress.

Lower. A town in Minangkabau, Sumatra. The heterogeneous crowd, varied clothing, busy market stalls, and iron roofs are typical of such scenes.

Press Assn., Royal Dutch Packet Navigation and American Museum of Natural History

PLATE 20

Upper. This Malaita village was built on an artificial island for defense against inland peoples.

Lower left. A Javanese in traditional dress of *batik* with *kris*.

Lower right. A tree house in a remote part of the Philippines. Isolated groups in remote forest and mountain areas of Malaysia and New Guinea have favored this type of architecture for security reasons.

Pan Pacific Press

PLATE 21

The modest "Mother Hubbard" dress, brought by missionaries to women of the South Seas, has been transformed by Hawaiians into a colorful *holoku,* gown with a train.

Philippine Bureau of Science and Press

Plate 22

Upper. Rural transportation in the Philippines. This is one of many styles of buffalo-, cattle-, and horse-drawn vehicles used in different districts of Malaysia today.

Lower. A bridge on a New Guinea trail. Native carriers played an essential part in getting ammunition and other supplies to front line troops over some of the roughest terrain in the world.

By contrast some groups live back from the shore because their traditional enemies have come by sea from adjacent islands. No sign of habitation may be seen at all along the beach, and their settlements may be carefully hidden deep in the bush where they are approached by narrow and easily defended trails. A flier passing over inland Borneo or New Guinea, for example, will see the scattered hamlets and clearings of such secretive peoples. Farther back in the mountains, groups may choose instead to place their villages on exposed ridges or crags, from which their guards may watch the surrounding countryside. Villages may still have defensive walls of dense plant growth, wooden stakes, or stonework. The marks of former warfare obviously continue to be heavy upon the living habits of many peoples, especially in Melanesia and the more isolated parts of Malaysia. Most elusive of all are the remnant groups of Negritos and other nomadic forest peoples, whose homes are the shifting campfires and rough bark or leaf shelters of their successive stopping-places.

In modern times, government authorities and missionaries have persuaded some of the more scattered-out groups to abandon their traditional types of settlement, and to build substantial villages in accessible spots. Often these villages are well laid out, with neat paths, hedges, and perhaps flower gardens. Most of the islanders, however, hold tenaciously to their traditional living sites. Here they feel the security of belonging, of being among friendly people and dealing with familiar supernatural forces; here, too, their ancestors are buried, sometimes right within the villages or even under the houses. Away from this locality they will always feel strangers, and generally be treated as such.

A visitor should be circumspect about going into a native settlement. He should try to give warning of his approach by sending a native messenger ahead, or letting himself be seen by the villagers, though usually they will have heard long before of his presence in the neighborhood. Often it is best to stop for a while outside the settlement, or at least to approach slowly, so as to give time for a reception committee of the officials and elders to gather. He should try to find out the correct place where visitors are entertained. If there is an extra-large building in the village, the space in front of it is frequently the traditional reception place or square. Nowadays villages may have a government office or schoolhouse built more or less in western style, and he can proceed to this center. At times a settlement may be taboo to visitors because of some ceremony or religious festival, and a stranger who forces his way in may arouse bad feeling. It is best, if at all possible, to find out beforehand what local custom is on such matters, and to have a reliable native guide and helper.

HOUSES

As in western countries, native house architecture is highly conventionalized. In theory it should be possible for a shipwrecked person or other visitor to know just where he is in the islands by the style of houses he sees. Actually this would be impossible because of the very great variety in house structure; not even scientists have recorded all the different styles.

Some peoples spend a minimum of effort on their houses, being content with small huts and hardly any furniture. Among the nomadic forest peoples they are rarely more than a lean-to. In an emergency the traveler may have the chance to find out how easy it is to make a reasonable shelter in the tropics, where bamboo, palm trunks, leaves, and coarse grasses are usually on hand as building materials.

Other groups lavish great efforts upon their houses, making them of heavy lumber or of elaborately plaited materials, and perhaps adding sculptures or other ornamentation. The remarkable houses of the Sumatran Minangkabaus and Bataks, for example, are works of art. Such houses are usually lived in for generations, and building one of them becomes a major event in the life of the community. In New Guinea, Borneo, and certain other areas there are groups among whom all the people in a settlement live in one huge house, each household having its suite.

The most general custom, however, is for a village to have a number of smallish family houses and one or more large buildings upon which the architectural effort of the group has been concentrated. These special houses may be the dwellings of chiefs or aristocrats, but frequently they belong to the community as a whole. A house of this kind is likely to be the center of religious life as well as a social gathering place. Often women are forbidden to enter, except perhaps at times of high ceremony, so that such a structure is frequently called a "men's house." Obviously the visitor seeing a special building of this kind should not try to enter it until he finds out what it is, and what beliefs the people hold regarding it. He should wait for an invitation, and once inside, should go only where his hosts indicate.

In the western Pacific and eastward to the New Guinea area, the island houses are usually raised up on piles or posts. This can be easily understood in view of the wet and swampy terrain of most of the rainy tropics, the protection afforded against harmful animals, and the greater ease of defense. In the interior forests, houses may even be placed partly or wholly in trees, sometimes thirty or more feet from the ground, with a ladder or notched pole which may be raised up to keep out intruders. In central and east Java, and here and there in other islands of the western Pacific, house structures are placed directly on the ground or on built-up stone or earth platforms. This is the characteristic building method in eastern Micronesia, the New Caledonia and Fiji sections of Melanesia, and the Polynesian islands. According to the local styles, houses may be rectangular, square, round (as with the traditional bee-hive huts of New Caledonia), oval, or many-sided. They may have sharp peaked or low pitched roofs, and the sides may be closed in or open, with perhaps Venetian-like blinds of plaited coconut leaves, or again not visible at all as the house is built wholly underneath the overhanging eaves of the roof.

Around the towns and ports, western building materials and architecture have set their marks on native housing, with results not always fortunate. Indeed, the traveler's first impression of a native village, gained in such an area, may be anything but pleasant. Hot tin roofs, walls made partly of beaten-out cans or sacking, and a general slummy appearance are likely to be the rule. Native sultans or chiefs have sometimes adopted western-style architecture with results varying from the highly artistic to the incongruous. Where natives take over elaborate western housing or furnishings this is likely to be less a matter of new tastes than of the prestige value among their fellows of owning western goods. A native chief whose home is full of modern furniture may sleep not on the bed or sofa but on the floor with a native-style mat and headrest.

The plan of house structures in a settlement is worth examining to see what ideas lie behind it. The living quarters of a household sometimes consist of several separate buildings. Some peoples, as in Polynesia, have taboos against cooking in a house, and so build separate cooksheds. Other structures may be for storage or for sacred purposes. The village buildings may be placed in an apparently haphazard way, or laid out in regular streets, possibly ranged around a central court which may serve as a ceremonial meeting place and dance ground. Occasionally each living unit is shut within its own wall or fence to keep livestock under control or to give privacy. There may be altars and fireplaces for sacrifices outside each house. Some peoples like to keep their dead relatives close at hand, as already indicated, and so bury them under cairns within the villages or beneath their houses, or even in stone coffins placed in prominent spots. But more usually a burial place is hidden at some distance from the village, or the bodies of the dead may be burnt or exposed for birds and other animals to dispose of. A family which has consistent bad luck when living on a certain houselot may take the house down and rebuild it on another site.

The inside of a native house may seem bare to western eyes. That is because activities go on, not at table and chair level as in a western home, but on low platforms or on the floor. The general plan of a house is usually apparent from a brief look around—the reception area for visitors, the cooking section if there is an indoor hearth, the storage and sleeping sections, and probably any religious shrine or sanctuary. Even if the house consists of only one room, the native mind will count it as divided up into compartments just as clearly as if it had a whole series of different rooms, and a person has a kind of ceremonious privacy in his own area even if he is actually visible. The house will be separated not only in terms of different uses but also according to the status of the people using it—this part, perhaps, for females, this for juniors, this for the elders, and this for guests. A visitor should never wander around casually inside a native house. He is almost certain to land in trouble by breaking some rule or touching a sacred object, and so giving offense to the people. Instead he should learn the correct local etiquette for approaching and entering the house, where and how to sit down when he gets inside, and whatever else native manners dictate. These people are just as sensitive about callers behaving properly in their houses as are Westerners, and the latter will not expect visitors to come in through the coal cellar, or appreciate having a stranger poke around in bedroom closets.

Native-style sleeping accommodation is sometimes very uncomfortable to anyone not brought up to it from childhood. Some islanders sleep in a small recess in the wall of their houses, or on a narrow wooden plank, or even in a box with a fire of glowing embers if the nights are cold. Yet villages accustomed to entertaining white men may surprise the visitor by making up a soft bed of mats, or possibly bringing out embroidered sheets and pillows which have been made on sewing-machines at the mission school.

If an outsider expects to stay any length of time in a native community, it is best to get the people to erect special buildings for him or his party. The governments have usually had resthouses built at all important settlements for the accommodation of visiting officials. In the Japanese-occupied areas, however, these structures have probably fallen into disrepair or have become too dirty to be pleasant.

CLOTHES

The island peoples, like Westerners, are very conventional about dress, and one may soon learn to recognize where natives come from by the style of their clothes, ornaments, hair-dos, and headgear. Even the scantiest kinds of garments such as loincloths may vary amazingly in their details from district to district. The clothing and ornaments an individual wears may give useful clues as to his status—whether he is an aristocrat or a poor man, an important person or otherwise. Clothes serve as symbols as well as body coverings.

Most natives have long since adopted the use of cloth garments. Yet in the more remote areas such as the back country of New Guinea, the Solomons, and the New Hebrides, and in the high mountains and deep forests of the Netherlands Indies and Philippines, the people are still likely to wear their traditional types of clothing, made of such materials as bark cloth, grass, or woven fiber, and often dyed in conventional colors. Some of these natives look barbaric enough, with scanty gee-strings, or perhaps penis sheaths made of bark, gourd, horn or shell. Their bodies may be tattooed or scarred, their ear-lobes stretched and pierced to hold large ornaments, and their noses plugged or skewered with a "spritsail" stick or quill. Sometimes the end of a loincloth hangs down behind, a native style which apparently gave rise to the popular but quite untrue story that some peoples of the region have tails. Women may wear long or abbreviated skirts or girdles, or sporran-like back and front coverings. A few isolated forest peoples traditionally wear no clothing, at least in the sense of garments for protection or for modesty, having at most a few ornaments for decoration.

Native dress materials, being neither so comfortable nor so durable as manufactured cloth, tend to go the way of the white man's homespun. Yet native groups, when they adopt cloth, manage to create distinctive styles of their own. The simplest is some form of waistcloth such as the Indonesian *kain* or *sarong,* and the South Sea *lap-lap, lavalava,* or *pareu.* This will have a conventional length, often nearly down to the ankle, and sometimes a conventional color scheme. One of the easy tricks which Westerners can learn from natives is how to twist in the ends of a waistcloth, or of an ordinary bathtowel, so that it will stay up of itself. Natives now frequently wear belts, preferably well ornamented, but these may be more for pleasure and prestige than for support.

In some Mohammedan areas of the western Pacific, long trouser styles are customary for men. Usually they are narrow at the ankle and sometimes they are quite tight around the legs. "Shorts" may be worn under a waistcloth, and nowadays they are increasingly used by men as the only lower garment, particularly for the ordinary round of daily work. Some conservative natives, however, dislike their young men adopting trouser styles as "aping the white man" or as definitely immoral. In the British Pacific islands the governments and missions have done their best to discourage the wearing of trousers by natives. If an upper garment is worn by men, it is usually a singlet. But shirts, neckties, and western or native-style jackets may be worn for special occasions, particularly by native leaders who reinforce their prestige by imitating their white rulers.

Women's dress made of cloth shows wide variety, from the long and shapeless Mother Hubbard introduced to the South Seas by the missions to two-piece styles of garment used widely in Malaysian areas, with the top often in jacket form and sometimes looking like what the Westerner would consider lingerie. In some places the women wear a short dress with a waistcloth as a supplementary lower garment, or a waistcloth only, with no upper garment. Even in villages under considerable western influence the women may discard their upper garments for comfort, provided no white man is around. When a woman's dress covers the upper arms and has a high neckline, it is often a sign that the people are Catholic converts. In the Philippines the top garment may be made of transparent fiber which shows the underclothing beneath, and a voluminous type of skirt and train is worn hitched up at one side, also revealing the undergarments.

The hair arrangement and headgear of both men and women often give clues to their home locality. Sometimes they are very elaborate, especially in the New Guinea area. Men with their hair cut short may be converts to Christianity, or at least be considerably adjusted to civilization; correspondingly persons who are conservative may indicate this by keeping their hair long. Many South Sea islanders treat their hair with lime so that it becomes blond to flaming orange in color, and native men as well as women may wear flowers in their hair. The Islamic peoples customarily wear a turban, with folds and knots peculiar to their own localities. In the Indies a black cap is particularly favored by supporters of the local nationalist movement. Except in the Christian Philippines, shoes or sandals are rarely used by natives, as their tough rubbery-soled feet can go without damage over sharp coral or lava. Shoes are another mark

*Netherlands Information Bureau, Auckland Weekly News, N. Z.
and Captain Frank Hurley*

PLATE 23

Upper. This Karo-Batak house in Sumatra is the home of sixteen families. Alongside it is the general burial place.
Lower left. Maoris of New Zealand dance the *haka*. Their girdles are of reeds dyed with black bands.
Lower right. Interior of a men's house or sacred community building in south Papua, 70 feet high at the entrance and 380 feet long.

Matson Navigation Co. and American Museum of Natural

PLATE 24

Upper. In a Samoan village the ceremonial hostess, with headdress and valuable mat skirt, dances with her attendants, who are wearing *tapa* or bark cloth. The beehive houses have open sides with blinds of coconut leaf.

Lower. In Tonga only persons of chiefly rank were allowed to play the billiard-like game called *lafo.* For a commoner to play it would in former days have brought the penalty of death.

of prestige, and they are likely to be worn only in aristocratic families or by native officials of the urban centers. Umbrellas may also be carried as a symbol of status. Where tattooing has important religious meanings, it may still be practiced, though sometimes such decorations may be on the hips or other parts of the body where it cannot be seen; otherwise it tends to die out along with other exotic types of adornment.

Health authorities in many parts of the tropical Pacific look with concern upon the wearing of modern-style garments, as frequently such clothing becomes dirty and unsanitary, or the people wear far too many clothes. They may also keep wet garments on instead of changing them. All this aids the spread of disease, especially of pneumonia and tuberculosis. The wearing of upper garments by women has been a subject of controversy, with the missions raising the moral issue; in Papua the government has gone so far as to prohibit by law the use of top coverings for women except by special permission or among such women as native pastors' wives and those living in the towns. Children in the island areas usually go more or less bare until they are seven or eight years old. In districts occupied by the Japanese, cotton goods have become so acutely short that doubtless many people have had to wear less clothes and to go back to their older bark, leaf, and fiber materials. Undoubtedly this lack of cloth is one of the main sources of grievance against the Japanese, and Allied troops are finding cloth a most useful article for trade and for making payments to natives for services.

As with the white man's Easter parades, festivals give the islanders their main chance to show off their wardrobes. Christian and Mohammedan natives put on their best clothes for their weekly religious services and especially for the holidays of their faiths. But it is when their own traditional ceremonies occur that the people put on a really spectacular show. At such times western-style or cloth garments may be discarded, and all their own finery, plus modern embellishments, comes to light. Like Scots putting on their kilts or American Indians their buckskin and feathers, the natives will bring out treasured clothing and ornaments, often highly decorated and artistic. For a major occasion they may spend weeks or months making masks, headdresses, or other festive gear, or else such paraphernalia may be unearthed from taboo recesses of their sacred god-houses. They may paint and primp until the results exceed the wildest imaginings of a Hollywood property man. Along with traditional native ornaments of shell, bone, feathers, and perhaps even gold, may be noted more familiar objects such as a string of bottle-caps, or coins, mirrors, and metal bells. Around the port towns, natives are used to putting on shows of this kind for tourists, but they are best seen at genuine native ceremonies.

TOOLS AND UTENSILS

In isolated places one may come across an islander carrying such a traditional tool or weapon as a club, spear, or bow and arrow. But only in a few remote districts in the Melanesian area will stone adzes and other tools be found still in use, to give a reminder that the island peoples outside Malaysia had no metals until the whites arrived. Nowadays steel tools such as knives, slashers or machetes, axes, scissors, and needles have become an essential part of the equipment of practically all accessible native households. In Malaysia, where the use of iron and brass has been known since the days of early contact with India and China, the local metalsmiths beat out knives, axes, and other tools in many conventional shapes which the newcomer may learn to recognize.

A native home today is likely to have an odd assortment of gear, partly of local make and partly bought at the store. Alongside a native-style food-bowl may be an enamel basin, some cheap chinaware cups, or that very precious commodity

HOME CONDITIONS   99

in native eyes, a five-gallon can. In a corner may be a wooden chest, possibly a fly-proof safe, and even a sewing-machine. Yet the day's rice may still be pounded with a wooden pestle and mortar, and food served on a plaited mat. Native life is in a state of transition, and every household in a village may have some different combination of the old and the new.

Frequently an article of traditional type, abandoned for ordinary use, will be produced on ceremonial occasions. At such times the household head may bring out from the family treasures an ancient carved bowl, or a chief may flourish some wicked-looking weapon from antiquity. The traveler must not be disappointed, however, if he has to wait until he gets to a museum back home to see what the old-time equipment of many of these island peoples was really like.

TRAVEL AND TRANSPORT

Away from the few urban and industrial centers the principal "roads" are still the sea and the inland waterways. The peoples who live along the coasts and the larger rivers and lakes are usually, though not always, good boatmen. Those who reached and settled the small islands of the open ocean are almost invariably expert navigators, as indeed they had to be to get to such places and to win a living there.

A person may find it extremely useful at times to be able to recognize some of the different sizes, shapes, and rigs of native vessels, so as to be able to identify at a distance the people in them. Even in a small area a number of distinct styles may appear, in the cut of bow and stern, the shape of sails, and the type of paddles. Seafaring peoples usually lavish great effort on the building and decoration of their more important craft, and as with other treasured wealth their manufacture and use tend to be surrounded with rituals and taboos about which the people are very strict. It may readily be understood why so hazardous an activity as navigating the open ocean should become saturated with elements of religion and magic.

The big *praos* of Malaysia, like the junks of China, can carry loads of considerable size. These native vessels may or may not have outriggers, but nearly all the smaller canoe types do. Usually the outriggers are single, that is, they extend to one side only, but sometimes double outriggers are used, a type of construction found most often in the western Pacific. An outrigger gives balance, and enables a canoe hull to be quite narrow in beam. This is a factor of great importance on islands where there are no trees with large trunks and such craft have to be made from small planks lashed and caulked together. Well worth noting are the amazingly different ways which local groups have worked out to attach an outrigger, using booms and perhaps struts of various shapes.

An alternative to the outrigger is to have a double canoe, with two hulls and a cross platform between. Craft of this style, such as the big *lakatois* of the Port Moresby region in Papua, are able to carry bulky cargoes in surprisingly shallow water. They also tend to have greater stability, as an outrigger canoe may upset in gusty or rough weather through the outrigger dipping too deeply or lifting out of the water. Where peoples have to go through heavy surf they may build a high superstructure on which to keep their goods dry. A useful craft for military or other transport may be made by joining two native canoes with cross pieces, constructing on top a platform of the size desired, and attaching an outboard motor.

Some native groups living on calm lagoons, swamps, or rivers dispense altogether with balancing devices, especially if they have large trees available to hollow into dugouts. Often, however, it takes experienced native boatmen to keep such single canoes from capsizing. Rafts are regularly used in a few places, and may always be built from light forest timbers or bamboo in an emergency. When passing through rapids, natives may attach bamboo or other buoyant materials around the sides of a canoe.

The islanders have sometimes modified the traditional styles of their vessels after seeing the white man's boats. The long whaleboat seems especially to have stimulated the ideas of native builders, and a boat of this style may be constructed, but perhaps made much longer and an outrigger attached. Manned by a double row of paddlers or rowers, or rigged with a sail, it can carry fifty or more people and go at a fast clip. Occasionally individual natives or whole settlements may own western-style craft—small sailing schooners, auxiliary ketches, or even launches. Nowadays nearly all the small vessels which carry on the minor inter-island trade are manned by native crews, and many have skippers who are native or part-native. Around most of the island ports there are native pilots who are thoroughly familiar with the local reefs and channels.

Native-style land travel is usually by foot trails, called "tracks" in the South Pacific. Unless such trails have been maintained and improved by the villagers under government supervision, as many are in normal times, they are for the most part in execrable condition. Tropical rains, steep terrain varied by swampy flats, frequent stream crossings, and the humid gloom of the forest make travel on them unpleasant for the white man. But the native traveler is used to such trails. His tough bare feet carry him nonchalantly over the roughest country, and he will cross a chasm on a single log or a swaying bridge of rattan. He can carry a sixty-pound pack all day, though it is usual to limit a carrier's pack to forty pounds. In the New Guinea region the success of Allied campaigns has been in no small degree made possible by the labor of such native carriers over trails of the worst possible type.

Government public works departments have sometimes built wire-reinforced bridges over difficult stream crossings on the main trails, as with the famous Wairopi ("Wire-rope") bridge in the Buna region of Papua. They have also maintained canoe-ferry services for the foot traveler, or even large rafts for vehicles, at river crossings. A district nearly always has officially established pay scales for carriers, boatmen, and other helpers. When using carriers for long trips in the interior of the large islands, the serious problem arises of providing food, as living off the country is possible only to a limited extent. Even if a carrier's pack were to consist entirely of rations, he would eat his own load in twenty-six to thirty days. Government parties and mining or other private expeditions have usually met the problem by establishing base camps at key points to which supplies could be transported by river or by plane. Where trail conditions are suitable, pack animals may sometimes be obtained, such as horses, oxen, or the slow but sure water-buffalo.

7. Social Customs

The pacific island peoples, living together in their local groups, have to meet essentially the same social problems that western families and communities do. They have to fit in the young and the old, regulate the contact of the sexes, bear and rear children, dispose of the dead, and handle many other matters of group concern. But they do so in ways often utterly different from those familiar to the white man, so that at times the latter may be hard put to understand them. To the people themselves, however, such ways are normal and right, backed by the authority of the ancestors and the approval of the deities. To them the social customs of the white man seem correspondingly outlandish, amusing, and in some respects immoral.

The first impression a visitor receives in going into an island community is whether its population is small or large. If a settlement has only ten or twenty houses, the natural assumption to make is that it has only a few dozen inhabitants. This may be true by western census standards; yet to the native the situation may be very different. Perhaps by his interpretations his ancestors are there too, together with numerous spirits and deities which affect his life. Contrary to the white man's estimate, the settlement is to him quite crowded, as both the dead and the supernatural powers may be in his mind a real part of the community. In such a place the visitor will have to be careful not to offend these unseen members of the group if he wants to keep the friendship of the people.

As an outsider gets to know a native settlement better, he

finds that it is in many ways like a small community back home. The people are busy with their local concerns, and everyone knows everyone else's business. Because the members of the group have lived together since childhood, they are likely to know one another intimately, yet there is plenty of room for gossip, rumor, jealousy, and rivalry. The people watch over one another's conduct, and woe betide any individual who fails to conform. A newcomer does well to feel his way slowly in establishing contacts with such a group, taking notes of its feuds and factions, and being careful not to get in with the wrong crowd and so to spoil his most important and useful contacts.

HOUSEHOLD AND FAMILY

The basic unit of social life in any island community, as with humans the world over, is the small group that lives together in a household. Among nomadic forest peoples the corresponding unit would be the group that shares the same shelter or campfire, while for the sea gypsies it would be the persons living on the same boat. This is the really intimate circle—the people who eat together, bring up the children, and share the common day-to-day round.

The Westerner calls this unit a family. Yet "family" is a deceptive label, because a group of this kind may not consist of a father, a mother, and children, as in western custom. Sometimes it may, but more usually the household contains a considerably larger number of relatives who live together in an "extended family." It may include three or more generations, with perhaps several brothers or sisters and their children in the group, much like a family in the Old Testament. Sometimes, if who's who in the home is tracked down, there are much greater surprises.

Instead of a man bringing his wife home to the parental

roof, or setting up a house unit of his own when he marries, he may as a husband have to go to live with his wife's kin group —a "matrilocal" or mother-locality type of family arrangement. His children may not inherit property or status from his own kin lines, but rather from his wife's kin ("matriliny"). A husband may have his main responsibilities not toward his own children but instead toward those of his sisters, while his own children look to his wife's brothers as a Westerner does to his father. A few societies in Malaysia and Melanesia carry this so far that a husband never lives with his wife and children, and he may only be able to visit with his wife secretly at night or outside the village. She lives with her kinsmen, and he stays with his, or lives in a separate men's house.

In many parts of the Pacific a husband is allowed to have more than one wife; and in at least one, the Marquesas Islands far to the east, a wife may have several husbands. Yet the proportion of people who indulge in such multi-marriage is usually very small. Only a sultan, chief, or aristocrat is likely to be able to afford more than one wife. The Mohammedan law allows a person to have up to four legal wives, and any additional consorts have the lower status of concubines. The first wife's children normally have a senior position, those of the second are next in importance, and so on down. In such a "polygynous" ménage all the women may live under one roof, or each may have separate quarters.

Occasionally a group has some kind of approved marital lend-lease system by which husbands and wives are swapped around. In some societies divorces are frowned on, especially if children are on the scene, because a main feature of family life is to provide a stable setting in which to bring up children. Others may allow marriages to break up casually, particularly if the couple have no living children or if there is a large kin group to care for any offspring. A girl may have had several husbands by the time she is twenty. Many groups adopt children back and forth from one family to another much more freely than Westerners do.

One of the high spots in the social calendar usually comes when the son or daughter of a sultan or chief gets married. Crowds assemble, feast-food is heaped high, and valuable property may be displayed and passed between the family groups concerned. At the other extreme, couples of the lowest class may merely need to live together to be recognized as married. In some cases the bride and groom may never have seen one another before, being from different districts, but nearly always they are from the same little local group in which people have been marrying together for centuries. Custom may even require formal marriage only after children have already been born to prove the union fertile, or, as in the Mentawei Islands west of Sumatra, not until children are grown up enough to support their parents.

Young people generally have some say as to whom they marry. Yet, much more than Americans would like, their families do the arranging in many societies. After all, a wedding creates a whole network of new "in-law" relationships, and in these intimate communities the relatives want to have a hand in the choice. As a result, romance, good looks, and even age may be less important in matching a husband and wife than social position, wealth, industriousness, and the desires of kin groups to make desirable connections. Many peoples, especially in the Melanesian region, go so far as to have direct rules defining just whom a person shall marry. A widespread custom is for a man to marry a daughter of his mother's brother. Another system is for men of a certain clan to get their wives from another fixed clan; perhaps one man in each gives over a sister in marriage to the other.

A formal marriage is usually surrounded with religious rituals that put the stamp of approval of the deities upon the match. It is also cemented with passing of property and other ceremonies involving the kin groups concerned. These activities dramatize the setting up of new family and in-law relationships, and serve as a sort of insurance that everyone, including husband and wife, will do their best to carry out the obligations they are incurring. Marriage "payments" in this region are usually heavier from the man and his family to the family of the girl—so-called "bride-price"—in contrast to the European custom of giving a dowry with the bride. Important families often betroth their children years ahead, and by keeping marriages within their own group they consolidate their position as an upper class or caste.

KIN AND CLAN

Kinship may be looked upon as the core of social relations in these communities, for all the island peoples lay great emphasis upon their kin connections. It is eminently useful for a person to have a wide range of relatives upon whom he may count for cooperation and support, provided of course he in turn treats them rightly. Out from every individual extends a network of kinsmen by birth, marriage, and perhaps adoption. This was so, too, in western society until or two three generations ago when modern industrial conditions brought a scattering out of population and wider kin connections tended to wither away.

Local custom carefully defines what behavior should be shown toward each type or class of relative, such as members of the immediate family, brothers of one's mother, brothers of one's father, grandparents, and parents-in-law. Toward some of them a person is respectful and restrained, and may have prescribed duties, while with others he may be free-and-easy, or be able to give orders. The eldest son in a family is frequently given special privileges, and may become later the senior elder or chief of his group, looked up to by his juniors but having in turn to support and care for them. A native who is working with a white man can usually assemble a group of his kinsmen if additional manpower is needed, and some of them are likely to be hovering around when he gets his pay.

Kin connections are remembered not only among the living but also back into the past, sometimes for many generations. The Polynesian peoples, for example, keep a careful record of their genealogies, and important families trace their ancestry back to ancient heroes and even to the gods. Such family trees are socially useful, just as they are in certain circles of Boston, Richmond, and the European capitals. A Polynesian captured in battle might save his life by proclaiming some kin connection with his captors. Many groups, including the Polynesians, take account of their lineages back through both their fathers' and their mothers' lines of ancestry. They are spoken of as "bilateral" or "two-sided" in their kinship reckoning.

Another widespread method of organizing kin connections is a so-called "clan" system. Here a "unilateral" or "one-sided" principle is emphasized by which descent is traced through either the father's line (patriliny), which is familiar to Westerners because European family customs are of this type, or the mother's line (matriliny). In groups with a patrilineal clan system, all males and their children are members of the clan, but females marry out in each generation so that their children are counted members of their husbands' clans. The opposite is true under a matrilineal clan system, and gives rise to some of the strange family arrangements which have already been described. Sometimes the name "gens" (plural "gentes") is given to a patrilineal clan. Clan members share a common tradition, and join together in ceremonial and other activities prescribed by local custom.

The religious beliefs of some peoples are such that the clan groups regard themselves as related to animals, plants, or other objects of nature, which become their "totems." Totemism is particularly widespread in the Melanesian region, and most peoples holding such ideas do not destroy or eat their totem animals or plants. Clans may also be grouped into larger clusters, called "phratries" (from the Greek word for "brother"), or into two complementary units called "moieties" or "halves," so that in the latter case the society concerned is said to have a dual organization. The questions to ask about any such institution as a clan, phratry, or moiety, in order to find out its meaning and use to the people, are "What does this institution do? What social, political, economic, religious and other ends does it serve?"

Nowadays, under the influence of governments and missions, and of contact with western ideas generally, there is a tendency for the family life of the islanders to become more like that of the white man. This is happening particularly around the towns, among the younger people who have been to school, and among persons holding western-type jobs. The ties of the immediate family are being strengthened, while the wider kinship bonds with their traditional privileges and duties are weakening. In this they are following along the same general lines of change as western societies. The more exotic customs are likely to disappear gradually, including polygamy, which can have little appeal for young women as they become educated and grow aware of an alternative form of marriage.

YOUTH AND AGE

Births and deaths come very often in these island communities, and cause far less shock and excitement than they do among white people. Because the population turns over more rapidly, the proportion of children and young people is nearly always larger than would be found in white communities, and very old people are correspondingly scarcer. It takes an exceptional individual to survive to old age in this rugged setting of life, and one can understand why such persons are given respect and honor, and may be thought to have the "inside track" as regards the favor of supernatural powers.

Age plays a highly important part in determining a person's status in the community. It is customary for the elders to assume the major responsibilities, while young people seem generally to be carefree even though they have to do a large part of the family and community work. The tasks of the elders are not easy, for land and other property have to be managed, work effort organized, religious duties carried out, and other affairs of the group directed. As a person grows up, he takes on increasing responsibilities and correspondingly he can give orders to those younger than he is. If an elderly person should be asked to get something done, he will most likely delegate the matter to someone younger and less important, and it goes on down the line until perhaps a small child finally carries out the assignment. One task which falls largely to elders is the training of their grandchildren in the local traditions—an economical way of transmitting expert knowledge and beliefs down through the generations. A young child will also receive a large part of his education from children a little older, especially a brother, sister, or other close relative who has to mind him while his parents are busy.

Some of the island societies have elaborate customs by which an individual is marshaled step by step up the ladder of age. Feasts may be given, property distributed, and other ceremonies performed at birth, when a child is given a name, at puberty, on "graduating" into the status of an adult, and later at death, burial, and perhaps for years after death. Many Melanesian groups have a long-drawn series of initiation rites through which children, especially boys, must pass to be accepted in adult circles. By western standards these rites may sometimes appear to be unnecessarily harsh, even cruel, but they dramatize for the initiates the responsibilities and privileges of adult life. Among Christian converts such traditional customs become more or less replaced by baptism, confirmation, and other rituals familiar in white society.

THE SEXES

The position given to men and women varies greatly in different societies. In the Philippines, a wife by tradition holds the purse-strings and in other ways has an influential say in affairs. By contrast, Melanesian women are often given a very subservient place by western standards, and may be shut out altogether from many of the religious observances and other important activities of the community. The island women frequently do heavy work which the white visitor would expect the men to be handling, such as cultivating the gardens and collecting firewood. Women and girls may not be allowed to eat until after the men, or at least the important men, have finished their meal.

Yet some over-hasty judgments may be made here. Even when women seem to be greatly subordinated to men, they have their own spheres in which they take full responsibility and get opportunities for leadership and for enjoyment. The islanders make a clear distinction between men's and women's activities, and both are essential to the community. The Westerner meets with surprises here as in other customs. Cooking, for example, is a man's job in some societies, and a father may do a considerable amount of baby tending. As in western societies today, the traditional work schedule of males and females is getting thrown out of balance, so that the division of labor is becoming less clear. Some tasks of men, such as fighting or making stone tools, have gone, while women's work may be heavier where families are larger or commercial crops are grown. Women are likely to age early in these places because of heavy work and frequent childbearing.

The island girls and women are just as concerned with catching the eye of the opposite sex as their more civilized sisters. Dances and festivals are usually their best opportunity to "shine," and even the elderly dames may take the chance to cut a figure. Yet native girls and women are likely to be timid and retiring when a stranger is around. They have much less chance than the men to travel and rub shoulders with outsiders, and so are generally less sophisticated. In remoter districts they may even hide at the first sight of a white man, though sometimes at the order of their menfolk.

The islanders in many places may seem to be very free in sex matters. One must not think, however, that there are no rules to the game. Every group has its own conventions of morality, even though they are often very different from those current in white society. Sex is too explosive, complicating, and disruptive a force to leave unregulated in any community. All peoples restrict the contacts of certain relatives of opposite sex who are bound closely by important social ties, such as members of the same family, and a group which may allow or encourage sex play and trial mating among the youth may have an absolute taboo against a brother and a sister so much as speaking to each other. Some of the island peoples, too, outdo the strictest Victorians in their prudishness. They may not even permit a husband and wife to show any signs of mutual affection in public. Such groups are particularly likely to resent any interference with their women.

Any stranger going into an island community will want to find out everything possible about such matters. Of course, if the local customs permit the women to be friendly with an outsider he will quickly be apprised of the fact.

R. H. Beck and Pan Pacific Press

PLATE 25

Upper. A Melanesian "sing-sing." Dancers with drums and festive ornaments at Madang, New Guinea.

Lower. The Hawaiian *hula;* one of the varied dance styles of the Polynesian peoples, though now strongly influenced by Broadway and Hollywood.

Scherpenhuyzen, U.S. Marine Corps and Netherlands Information E

PLATE 26

Upper left. The famous Balinese dancer Mario teaching a pupil. The highly stylized dances are accompanied by percussion instruments.

Upper right. Movies have a profound effect on the islanders. They are now seen by natives wherever our forces go.

Lower. The Javanese puppet plays (*wayang*), telling stories of gods and heroes from the ancient past of India as well as of Java, are for the masses a source not only of entertainment but also of moral teaching.

CLASS AND CASTE

The island societies show in some phases of their life a strong development of the democratic spirit. Decisions on current matters may be thrashed out through meetings and consultations of the family, clan, or community, in which all members may have their say. Every effort is made to reach a unanimous opinion, even if it entails long-drawn palaver, so that no dissenting minority will exist as a disturbing influence to mar group solidarity. This happens especially in the small self-contained social groups and communities in which everyone knows everyone else.

At the same time, there is a strong tendency for leadership and authority to become concentrated within some special class or élite which has superior prestige and status. Such a privileged group may get its power in many different ways. Its members may be the descendants of early conquerors from outside; or they may have risen up within the society itself by virtue of leadership in war, possessing ceremonial wealth, having special revelations from the deities, or being descended from the earliest settlers or from ancient heroes and gods by way of the senior family lines.

A group of this kind tends to perpetuate itself as an upper class by consolidating its power, surrounding itself with ceremony and symbolism, and marrying its members together. It may even establish rules which forbid its members to marry out, and which prevent outsiders from getting in, so that it becomes a closed corporation or caste.

In Malaysia the development of such class and caste distinctions received a strong impulse through contacts with the social system of India. Throughout many parts of the area there are entrenched aristocracies, and at their apex may be "royal" families from which the ruling sultans and rajahs are drawn. In the Philippines and in western Micronesia the Spanish methods of government favored the building up of the grandee class of landowners and political leaders called *caciques,* which has its counterpart in Latin American countries today. Farther east, the Polynesians have had an aristocratic type of society graded principally in terms of birth, with paramount chiefs of exalted rank and sacredness at the top. An American may find his democratic feelings ruffled at the pomp and ceremony which surrounds high-born people, and at the humble bowing and scraping that custom may require from the ordinary people.

At the opposite end of the social scale a class sometimes exists which Westerners would consider slaves. Slavery is an old practice in many of these island areas, being approved by the Islamic faith. The persons concerned might be captives of former wars, or they might have been enslaved because of debts. People may be born into the slave class generation after generation. Western governments have frowned upon this custom, yet even where formally eradicated by law it tends to persist in some type of permanent bond-service or tenancy. Between the royal families and the slave class there may be many rungs on the social ladder. Peasant families who own their own land, and persons who have an independent source of money income, would be about equivalent to the middle classes in western society.

Members of the aristocratic groups are usually furthest along in adopting modern customs. They may be seen in smart western clothes, skilled at polo perhaps, sending their sons to college, and thoroughly at ease when entertaining whites. Yet they tend to lean conservatively toward maintaining the status quo for the mass of their followers. At the other extreme the depressed groups are the potential source for social revolution as they gradually become articulate. It is no wonder that many conservatives fear education for the masses as a dangerous force, while nationalist leaders do everything possible to stimulate its spread.

ETIQUETTE

The island peoples nearly aways lay great stress on etiquette and ceremony. These oil the wheels of social relations, especially between persons who do not know one another intimately. The visitor finds that each group has its own code of good and bad manners. A native will not expect a stranger to know his etiquette, but he will be pleased, and often amused, when such a person tries to fit in. Even a little attention to this will carry quite a long way in good relations, just as it does in a western community.

The first item of etiquette worth getting to know, as mentioned earlier, is how to meet and greet people—the local equivalents of "good-day," shaking hands, and chatting about the weather. Nearly always there are special forms of politeness to be used toward persons of importance, such as headmen and religious leaders. If such persons are squatting or sitting, it is wise for a visitor to do the same before he speaks, in case he gives offense by talking down at them. Note should be taken of how people squat or sit, as such positions may be conventional. Where it is the custom to sit cross-legged, for example, stretching out one's own legs may be the height of rudeness. It is best never to lean over the head of a native, especially with food in the hands, as the head is counted very sacred among many of these peoples.

A ceremonious gift is frequently handed to a visitor as part of the local etiquette, perhaps some betel, eggs, a fan, or a piece of native cloth. It should be accepted with due politeness, and something should be given in return as opportunity offers, or better still a gift may be made first. A traveler may easily find out ahead of time what goods the local people will most appreciate, and if nothing else is available cigarettes are almost always acceptable. The ceremonious passing of tangible objects binds people together and gives public recognition of their good relations.

Eating and drinking are nearly always surrounded with etiquette and ceremony. A visitor being entertained by a native group can watch his hosts for a lead as to the local "table manners." A person's relations with the opposite sex, as indicated already, are always tied up with formal do's and don'ts, and what may be talked about in any given conversational circle has its borderlines of politeness. Performing the natural functions is perhaps everywhere surrounded by such customs. Some peoples are much more public about this than Westerners are, while others demand the greatest privacy. The latter is particularly so in sections of Melanesia where the people think that magic may be performed against them by way of anything which comes from their persons.

Natives frequently like to show that they know something about the white man's etiquette. They may offer to shake hands, or may produce knives and forks at a meal. The visitor should accept this in the same spirit that he would want the natives to show at his own attempts to follow their manners. If they do not know how to shake hands properly, so that their hand grip is flabby, or they trip over other customs, he should never laugh or otherwise show a ridiculing attitude. Nothing can more quickly short-circuit friendly feelings.

AMUSEMENTS

The islanders have various traditional sports and entertainments which they enjoy taking part in or watching. Among these may be local types of wrestling or boxing, sometimes highly formalized so that they are almost more like a dance performance than a sport. Games of skill frequently give a reminder of the old days of war, as with throwing spears for accuracy or distance, or trying to hit a moving object bowled along the ground. Some groups have native versions of parlor games, such as checkers or making string figures on the hands. The games played by native children are always interesting to watch, and they are often modeled upon the valued activities of adult life.

In Malaysian areas animal fights are often popular. Best known is cockfighting, which goes on in spite of government attempts to suppress it, but bulls and even fish or crickets may be matched in the same way. Such contests attract the sporty betting crowd, for these people are often enthusiastic and skilful gamblers. Among competitive sports are bull and horse races, and canoe races. Hunting and fishing, in addition to providing food, have their pleasure side as well—for example, catching sharks with a noose. Some coastal and river peoples are good swimmers and spend a great amount of time in the water, but others seem to dislike getting wet unnecessarily.

Many native groups have taken over western sports and amusements, at times adapting the rules to their own tastes. English cricket and soccer and rugby football are played widely, even in out-of-the-way parts of New Guinea where they might be least expected. It is astonishing to see how far natives can "boot" a ball with bare feet. In Papua the government gives soccer balls to native settlements, and the game provides something of a substitute for the former inter-village warfare. Recently a Fijian rugby team toured New Zealand and defeated the best local teams in that country; its captain was a grandson of the old cannibal chief Thakombau, once "king" of Fiji. In the Philippines baseball, volleyball, and boxing have enthusiastic followings. Western card playing and gambling games have been adopted by many natives. In the large town centers they may play tennis and golf, enjoy western-style dancing, become movie fans, and have their boys and girls in Scout troops.

For some native peoples the filling in of leisure time has become a serious problem. Their old warfare has stopped, and many of the arts, crafts, and religious ceremonies which formerly occupied their time have died out. In some of the Christian groups the missions have forbidden dances and other activities that smack of "heathenism." As a result, life in these confined little communities may become drab and uninteresting. Governments and missions have recently been trying to develop substitutes in the way of new amusements and interests, and also to encourage the revival of old arts and crafts, in order to fill the void. It is a problem somewhat like that leading to adolescent delinquency in many western communities.

Anything the visitor is able to do to entertain his native hosts will help to generate good feeling. If he has any novel articles he could show them around, and he could work up a contest in any sport or game, such as putting the shot or jumping. To sing a few songs should make a hit; probably the tunes of some of them will be known already to natives who have traveled. He may be able to add some parlor tricks on any festive occasion. Even if only the children and young people take part, the elders will be pleased and interested. The natives may not think the same things are amusing as the white man does, but they will appreciate the effort, and the visitor may suddenly find that he has scored a smash hit.

ARTS AND FESTIVALS

A close relation usually exists in native life between entertainment and religion. On occasions when people get together for important religious ceremonies, such as at the birth, marriage, or death of an important person, or after harvest time, they may include games, dances, theatricals, story-telling, and other entertainments as part of the proceedings. Traditional arts like carving, music, and dancing are strongly permeated with religious meanings. Where any people put a great amount of effort into some form of art, as for example making elaborate masks and headdresses, or having a highly formalized style of dance, it may be expected that these have some sacred meaning, and the outsider should be doubly careful not to interfere with such activities or to treat them lightly.

Some of the island peoples do a great amount of painting, carving, and weaving in elaborate patterns. In all such art they have their own standards of what is beautiful or ugly, sometimes very different from that of the white artist. Other peoples are not interested in these types of self-expression, so that their material equipment seems plain and matter-of-fact. All the islanders, however, appear to lay great stress upon music and dancing.

Native singing and chanting may take a little getting used to, particularly as the western ear may not be trained to catch all the nuances of sound which the native hears. The white man will understand native music best where the people have taken over the western scale and harmony for some of their songs, perhaps accompanying them with a guitar, ukulele, or mouth organ. Yet nearly always any western-style music is given a characteristic local form, sometimes long-drawn and rather mournful, sometimes highly staccato and vigorous. In many groups the traditional musical instruments are limited to a few basic forms such as drums and flutes, but others have a regular orchestra. The most elaborate type of music is the Javanese *gamelin* orchestra, which is made up chiefly of drums, gongs, and other percussion instruments.

Music is usually associated with dancing and theatricals. Melanesians, for example, love to get together for what is known in pidgin as a "sing-sing," in which they chant and dance for hours or even days, interspersing this with feasting and other ceremonious activities. In some Malaysian areas, highly trained troupes perform traditional dances and theatricals, in which every movement of head, hip, or finger has some meaning to the local audience. The heroes, villains, clowns, witches, and other figures which may be represented in such performances should be recognizable even to the stranger. In Java the people are also devotees of traditional puppet shows and shadow plays.

Native theatricals are usually built upon ancient stories and events, and besides giving entertainment they dramatize the moral values and character traits cherished in the local cultures. In the Philippines, so-called *moro-moro* shows put on by traveling players depict the struggles between the Christians and the Moors in old Spain, ending inevitably in Christian victories. Elaborate processions and other pageantry are often included in native celebrations, much like a Mardi Gras except for religious meanings which are usually involved.

Most native groups will welcome a white visitor on such occasions, provided he shows no disrespect. He will probably feel that native entertainment moves along at too slow a pace for his taste. Yet the long intervals give the people a chance to visit, gossip, flirt, and otherwise enjoy the change from their everyday round of living. To Westerners time marches on, where to most islanders it flows by. A big native celebration may have taken many weeks to prepare; it can be understood why the people get the most they can out of it, and are in no hurry. In addition to the larger festivals, native groups have many kinds of smaller family, clan, and community ceremonies that give zest to living and help the people over the rougher spots—at crises in the life of the individual, when luck is good or bad, and before, during, and after house-building, planting, fishing, and other vital activities. Thus life itself becomes drama.

Templeton Crocker

Plate 27

The traveller may come across old stone ruins in the forest or along the shore. Here such a place has been cleared on Nuku Hiva Island in the Marquesas. Usually local natives stand in awe of these relics of the past.

Netherlands Information Bureau and American Museum of Natural Hi

PLATE 28

Upper. A group of Balinese men performing a Brahman ritual on the shores of the island of Bali.

Lower. Ritual dance connected with cultivation of *taro*: Bellona Island in the Solomons. The gods are supposed to reside in the chief's house (in rear) during this series of rites.

Netherlands Information Bureau

PLATE 29

Upper. Mohammedan mosque at Medan, Sumatra.
Lower. Men's house and its stone platform among the Bontok mountain people in the northern Philippines. Not so long ago it was a center for headhunting ceremonies, and animal sacrifices are still performed here.

Netherlands Information Bureau and U.S. Air F

PLATE 30

Upper. Christian Indonesians attending church at Ende, on the island of Flores.
Lower. Dedication of a chapel built by the natives of Guadalcanal and presented to the United States of America as a memorial for the Americans who died in expelling the Japanese from the island.

8. Religion

PEOPLE ARE USUALLY more sensitive about religious matters than about any other aspect of their lives. For most of the islanders, religion is likely to mean considerably more than it does to the average white man. It covers not only their beliefs about such problems as the nature of deity and the hereafter, but also much of what Westerners call science, medicine, and philosophy. It represents their fundamental interpretations of the universe, and of their own place in it—the assumptions and verities upon which their life is founded.

It will therefore be wise for any visitor to find out all he can about the beliefs and practices of any groups among whom he goes, such as their ideas of the supernatural, their religious leaders, their sacred places and objects, and their rituals and taboos. Easy as this is to say, however, it is almost certain that these will prove the most difficult phases of native custom to get to know intimately. The white man would not be keen about opening up the intimacies of his faith to a stranger; and even if he were willing to do so, he might find difficulty in putting religious matters into words.

In some areas the task is made simpler because of the work of Christian missions. It may come at first as quite a shock to hear Christian hymns and to see the people attending church in some remote forest clearing or isolated island. Today, as indicated already, the Polynesians are practically all Christians, being adherents of churches or mission bodies such as the Roman Catholic, Methodist, Congregational, and London Missionary Society ("L.M.S."). The Micronesians, too, are mostly either Catholic, as are nearly all the people in formerly Spanish Guam and other western islands, or Protestant, as the majority of the Gilbert, Marshall, and east Caroline peoples. A minority of conservative Micronesians keep to their older local faiths, and so are classed by the church as "heathens" or "pagans."

The Melanesians have been converted to Christianity about in proportion to their contact with civilization. Groups such as the Fijians and New Caledonians have practically all been Christian for a generation or two. In the New Guinea, Solomons, and New Hebrides areas the peoples living along the accessible coasts and on the lower reaches of the rivers are likely to be converts. The twelve different mission bodies working in Australian New Guinea and the Solomons claim to have in all over a half-million adherents. Yet many Melanesian groups continue to hold to their local faiths, being either untouched as yet by missions or unconvinced that the beliefs of their ancestors should be discarded.

In Malaysia the religious picture is more complicated. The Filipinos of the north and central Philippines, comprising all but about one-twentieth of the population, have been Christians for over three centuries. The Philippines are thus unique in being the only dominantly Christian nation in the Orient. Nearly all these people are Catholics, but Protestant missions have made many converts among the "non-Christian" mountain groups in recent years. Large Christian communities also exist here and there in the Netherlands Indies. Most Ambonese and Minahasa people of the Moluccas and northern Celebes respectively have long been Protestants, while many of the Bataks, Dyaks, and other formerly "pagan" peoples in Sumatra, Borneo, and the Celebes have been converted by Protestant missions during recent decades. Catholic missions have had their greatest success in the Flores and Timor regions. All told, Protestant mission bodies in the Netherlands Indies claim to have about three-quarters of a million adherents, and Catholic missions a half-million. Yet the great majority of the Malaysians are of the Islamic faith, and in Bali and east Java the earlier Hindu (Brahman-Buddhist) tradition survives. Finally, in the remoter forest and mountain areas many groups keep to their ancient religions, resisting both Islamic and Christian encroachment so far as these faiths may have reached them.

THE LOCAL RELIGIONS

The traditional beliefs of native peoples are often called "superstitions." Such a term, however, along with "pagan" and "heathen," is best avoided by anyone who believes in the democratic idea of freedom of religion. Whatever the Westerner may think about the adequacy of native beliefs, the people concerned regard them as spiritual truth. Even rites and ceremonies which seem merely mumbo-jumbo make it possible for them to meet with confidence the difficulties and uncertainties of life. The visitor quickly gets to appreciate how closely their religion is linked with food production, maintaining law and order, treating the sick, and everything else of importance in the local round.

It is hard to find a general word to cover these native faiths, the more so because of the very great difference from group to group. They have sometimes been called "nature religions" because of the intimate relation that beliefs always have to the local conditions of nature. An agricultural people, for example, is likely to have its religion focused on the annual drama of producing its key crops; a maritime people, upon canoes and fishing; and a group in an arid zone, upon getting a good rainfall. Anything unusual or uncontrollable in nature, such as rainbows, storms, a volcano, or a man-eating crocodile or tiger, is given a supernatural interpretation. Birth, death, and the hereafter are always subjects for speculation, and all these religions lay great stress upon relations between the living and the dead—

keeping on good terms with one's ancestors, and avoiding harm from unfriendly ghosts. The worlds of these peoples are also populated with numerous deities and spirits, good and evil, helpful and harmful.

To grapple with these matters, the groups concerned employ many kinds of ritual, or religious acts. Each faith has its calendar of religious holidays and festivals that put people on spiritual alert. A widespread custom is to please the gods or consult the omens by making sacrifices of such animals as chickens, pigs, dogs, or water-buffaloes, and formerly of human beings in some regions. Where cannibalism and headhunting have been practiced they had religious meanings, and human skulls may still be found in the sacred places of communities more recently weaned from these customs. Seeing a pig dismembered in order to read the will of the deities from the condition of its liver and gallbladder may not be the white man's idea of a religious act, but if he watches the faces of the people he will see what it means to them.

It needs little emphasis that a stranger must be careful about breaking supernatural rules or trespassing in sacred places. Usually a community has one or more sacred structures, perhaps an elaborate building, or a stone-paved court or platform, and each home may have a shrine or hallowed spot. A widespread custom is to regard certain mountains, pools, trees, and groves as sacred. Natives would look upon interference with such places much as a church congregation would if a native visitor in a western country were to rummage around the altar of a cathedral. Sometimes images, standing stones, graves or tombs, altars, and hearths on which sacred fires are lit are located at these religious spots. A form of religious platform or court, known in Polynesia usually as the *marae,* is widely distributed. It takes many local forms, but often it has a raised altar with standing stones, and at times the stones are actually carved into the figures of ancestors or gods as with the great statues of

Easter Island. Those familiar with the beliefs and rites of ancient Greece and Rome will realize that many of these religious elements to be found in the islands had their counterpart in the ancient European world.

Anyone who wants to get the cooperation of the islanders will need to develop friendly relations as far as possible with the religious leaders in their communities. Such persons may be organized into some rather formal priesthood or society, but more usually they are individual experts (often called "shamans")—men and women who have been trained by their predecessors, or who have had special revelations from the deities. A village may have a number of these religious practitioners, some perhaps specialists in agricultural matters, some healers, some seers and prophets who look into the future, and some experts in different kinds of magic, including the black arts of sorcery.

Groups which have become Moslem, Hindu, or Christian, devout as they usually are in these imported faiths, still hold to many of their older beliefs. Local spirits and ghosts have easily found a place in the Pantheons of the new religions, and the people take no chances in supernatural matters. They are particularly likely to carry over the fear elements of the old religion, such as beliefs about evil spirits, ancestral and other ghosts, the magical arts, charms, omens, and taboos. A good Islamic community may sacrifice a water-buffalo and engage in some age-old ceremony relating to the local spirits, or Christians may call in a native "medicine-man" to deal with illness or a seer to interpret dreams. The fundamental spiritual assumptions and securities of a culture die hard.

MOHAMMEDANISM

The native peoples in Java and the Malay Peninsula are almost all Moslem, and so too are most Sumatrans, especially along the east (northern) coast. In Borneo and the Celebes the coastal peoples are usually of this faith. The so-called Moros ("Moors") of the southern Philippines have kept tenaciously to their Islamic religion in spite of generations of pressure from their Christian fellows farther north, and also doubtless because of such pressure. Farther east, in the Lesser Sundas, Moluccas, and New Guinea, the followers of the Prophet thin out, being confined mainly to the few port centers and to certain native states. The numerous sultans and rajahs in Malaysia usually trace their ancestry back in part to Mohammed, by way of the *sayyid* missionaries spoken of earlier, and their native realms and capitals are major strongholds of Islam.

The Mohammedan peoples are worshippers of Allah, whose will, they believe, was revealed to the Arabian Prophet in the early part of the seventh century A.D., and written into the sacred Koran or "Reading." Islam, the name given by Moslems to their faith, means "submission" (to the will of Allah). Islamic doctrines draw heavily upon both Hebrew and Christian scriptures, but are regarded by the faithful as being a further divine revelation beyond these earlier religions. The spiritual capital of Islam is Mecca, the birthplace of Mohammed and center of pilgrimage for the Moslem world. Thousands of Moslems from Malaysia make this pilgrimage annually in normal times, and those who have done so, called *hajjis,* may be recognized by their white turbans.

Mohammed, a camel-driver in his youth, had to leave his home town because of opposition to his preaching. His "Flight" or Hegira (*hijra*) to Medina in the year 622 marks the beginning of the Islamic calendar, or A.H. 1. In Medina he became head of the state, and from here the Mohammedan religion spread out through the Arabian and Mediterranean regions and across Asia. The Koran was put together after his death, and consists of Jewish and Arabian tradition and history, prophecies, moral precepts, and laws. It is arranged in chapters and verses, and is considered so sacred that a Mohammedan is angered to see it even touched by an unbeliever.

The Islamic doctrine stresses the oneness and austere righteousness of Allah, and the brotherhood and equality of all believers, or at least of all male believers, regardless of race or other differences. Women are given a humble position by Koranic doctrine. A good Mohammedan is expected to say five daily prayers, prostrating himself in the direction of Mecca at dawn, at noon, and three times around sunset. He attends services at his mosque on Fridays, performs ritual washings—in sand if water is not available—and gives alms, drinks no liquor, and keeps the Hebrew food taboos, especially regarding the uncleanness of pigs. He observes the Islamic calendar of religious festivals, notably the fasting month of Ramadan, high point of the Moslem year, during which he must eat nothing from dawn to dusk each day. If at all possible he makes a pilgrimage to Mecca once in his lifetime. He is supposed to obey the moral and legal codes set by the Koran, and administered by the Moslem elders and teachers who provide the leadership for this religion.

In actual practice the Islamic faith has been considerably adapted and even diluted as it has extended out to regions such as Malaysia. There are a few places where the people are very strict Moslems, notably in Achin at the western tip of Sumatra. Nearly all Malaysian Moslems, too, are quite assiduous in carrying out the formal duties of their faith, its public exercises and taboos, and they have great respect for Islamic teachers and for people of Arab blood. Yet the austere doctrines of the Prophet have been mellowed by the artistic, pleasure-loving Malaysians, and the legal codes of the Koran dealing with marriage, property, and other matters have made little headway where they run counter to the local *adat* or customary law. The

Minangkabaus of Sumatra, for example, have been Moslem for centuries, yet their matrilineal kinship system stands firm in spite of its utter contrast to the marriage, inheritance, and other rules of the Koran.

Islam thus forms something of a devout veneer upon the Malaysian way of life. In recent years, however, educated Moslems have been in contact with the more vigorous spirit of modern Islam, as found in Turkey, Arabia, and Iraq today, so that in places like Java this religion is undergoing something of a revival. The "don'ts" to be careful about among Moslems are mostly obvious. An outsider should never argue about their faith, enter or loiter around their mosques, interfere with their worship, offer them pork or alcohol, or swear, smoke, or spit in front of them. If he employs Moslems, he should not try to force them to work during their religious festivals.

HINDUISM

On the island of Bali, the people keep conservatively to a local type of Brahman religion, colored also by Buddhism. They have an elaborate round of ceremonies, including colorful temple pageantry, which has fascinated western artists and tourists. A visitor to their temple grounds must enter only by the narrow side gates, and should not go on to the platform or touch the images of the gods. These people have a taboo against eating beef products.

In east Java some of the hill people still cling to this older type of faith, once followed in that island. Its marks also show strongly in the art, theatricals, and poetry of the Javanese in spite of the Mohammedan overlay. Many old ruins in Java and Sumatra attest to the former hold of Brahman and Buddhist beliefs. On the nearby Asiatic mainland the Cambodians, Thais, and Burmese are Buddhists.

Pan Pacific Press

PLATE 31

Modern pageantry in the islands is still infused with the spirit of old traditions: the Hawaiian *lei* queen, named each May day, is accompanied by bearers of the *Kahili,* sacred feather emblems of old time chiefs, reproduced here in flowers.

U.S. Marine

PLATE 32

The island peoples may be expected in the future to take their full share in the affairs of their homelands. A Samoan marine here patrols the coast in American Samoa.

CHRISTIAN MISSIONS

How far the Christian faith becomes more than a veneer of formal behavior and belief among these island peoples depends upon the education of the persons concerned. Missionary work started as early as 1548 in the Moluccas, but most mission activity in the islands falls within the last century. Often the most devout Christians are found among recent converts along the frontiers of contact, especially if only one mission is working in the community so that they are not troubled by conflicting and competing doctrines.

Native Christians are usually strict about religious observances such as family prayers, baptisms, keeping the Sabbath, and attending church. In some places they have erected imposing cathedrals, and their local churches and chapels are likely to be important centers of social life, with frequent meetings, choir practice, schools for the children, and festivals and processions. Catholic traditions and customs imported from Spain and Mexico have become deeply rooted in the Philippines and western Micronesia; villages have their patron saints and their fiestas, and a ceremony such as All Souls night, when the people gather in the cemeteries and eat with the spirits of the dead, is a high point in the annual round. In Christian communities the traditional leaders have usually become the church deacons and elders, thus winning religious support for their authority as in the days of their former gods. Many an island patriarch is able to quote the Bible extensively, and orators will adorn their speeches with texts. Yet below the surface of devout observance old beliefs and customs tend to fuse in with the new.

All mission bodies have advanced schools or colleges in which they train selected natives as pastors, catechists, or teachers. Much of the dangerous spadework for present-day missions in warlike Melanesian areas was done by Fijian, Samoan, Tongan, and other native missionaries from the islands farther east, and natives in these islands have given large sums of money to develop the new mission fields. When white missionaries in northern Papua were forced to leave by government order at the time of the Japanese attack, such native mission workers sometimes kept the religious life of the people running smoothly. Thousands of men and women from the local peoples are also on the mission staffs. Native church leaders wield very great influence, and can give important help to a visitor. Most of them can read and write at least in the common language used by the mission. They have generally proved loyal to the whites in the face of Japanese invasion, cooperating with Allied forces and aiding flier's shot down in the battle zones, often at great personal risk.

The mission bodies have carried on health work and education, sometimes getting financial help from the government for these purposes. Some of them have plantation, industrial, and commercial enterprises, notably the large German missions in the New Guinea region. These are developed both to provide financial support and to give training to converts who naturally serve as the work force. Thousands of natives have received instruction in boat-building, carpentering, smithing, sewing, and other pursuits at the main mission centers. The newcomer may well feel startled, however, the first time he sees over a trading store a sign such as "Sacred Heart of Jesus, Ltd."

LOCAL SECTS

Besides these established faiths, native sects or cults of obviously modern origin have sprung up in the islands. Local prophets or seers have emerged to proclaim new revelations of truth, and have gained followings large or small. This has been taking place all along the frontiers of the world wherever people become skeptical about their traditional beliefs, yet do not fully accept the foreign religions brought in from overseas. In such an uncertain state of mind they are likely to try out any new religious or mystical cult which claims to have supernatural answers to their problems. Western countries, too, are no strangers to such tendencies.

At times native movements of this kind have a set of beliefs and rituals which show few outward signs of white influence, as with a famous cult called the "Vailala Madness" that broke out years back in the Gulf region of southern New Guinea. At the other extreme they may duplicate closely a western faith, mainly substituting native leadership, as with the Aglipayan Church in the Philippines, a native version of Catholicism. Usually, however, their prophets manage to work out some strange combination of the old and the new. In the Madang district of northeast New Guinea a cult called "Letub" developed recently which, through strange rituals that included dancing in graveyards at night, purported to unlock the secret of how the white settlers managed to get freight consignments without apparently having to work for them. Movements of this kind have sometimes become violent and have generated crusades to expel the white man; governments have had to suppress them by force. Yet it is only fair to realize that, however fantastic they may appear in western eyes, such faiths represent for the people concerned a genuine attempt to solve their problems and to answer the age-old questions which have brought men's religious thought into existence.

9. Closing Word

The materials presented to this point have brought into focus the fact that the islanders are thoroughly human people. They have the same general needs and interests, the same problems and anxieties, as the man of New York or London or the visitor's own home town. True, there is an important screen of cultural differences, of customs and ideas, which has been welded out in this other part of the globe. But the more intimately one gets to know the native as a person, and wins his friendship, the more such differences fade into the background.

The lives of the islanders, like those of the western peoples, are inevitably being changed under the impact of the modern machine age and the development of world communications. But many of the adjustments they must make are far more drastic than those faced by Westerners. In some matters they are having to adapt themselves within a few years to changes that in the white man's cultural development were spaced over centuries.

Any visitor will be challenged to speculate about what future lies ahead of these peoples, and what policies the controlling countries should adopt in political, economic, educational, and other spheres. The problems of the island areas will not be solved easily or quickly, even though many places are small. Different communities, and also the families and individuals within them, are strung out at all stages of change and of competence to care for themselves without help and supervision. In some respects the island peoples have already worked out about as good solutions as can be found for getting along satisfactorily in their island homes, and the visitor can learn much from them. In other ways they can profit tremendously through the new opportunities now being opened up.

One thing becomes clear to anyone who gets to know the islanders well, namely, that they have the full human potential for development and adaptation. Though isolated for so long from the main currents of civilization, they fabricated elaborate and satisfying modes of living within their local settings. Now that such isolation is breaking down, they are responding as fast as they become convinced that the new is better than their own—slowly in some things, rapidly in others. There is no scientific reason for assuming that they are en masse biologically inferior, any more than the Stone Age Britons were in Caesar's time.

Already, indeed, some groups and individuals who have had special stimulus are participating very fully in the heritage of modern civilization, and several outstanding persons such as Rizal have already had an influence beyond their local settings. Given time and opportunity, the island peoples should be able to expand their horizons and to make creative contributions to the world community.

APPENDIX A
Basic Information

Governing Country	Place	Form of Government	Area (Sq. Miles)	Principal Population Groups (Approx.)	
Australia	New Guinea	Mandated Territory	93,000	Native Chinese White	850,000 2,200 4,400
	Papua	Territory	90,540	Native White	350,000 1,800
Australia, Gt. Britain and New Zealand	Nauru	Mandated Territory controlled by Australia	9	Native Chinese White	1,900 1,400 200
Chile	Easter	Dependency	50	Native	500
France	New Caledonia and Loyalties	Colony	8,000	Native White Asiatic	30,000 18,000 12,000
	Wallis and Horne Society Is.	} Establishments of Oceania	59 657	Native Chinese White	6,500 27,500 4,500
	Tuamotus and Gambiers		330	Native Chinese	1,200 6,800
	Australs Marquesas		70 490	Native Native	300 3,200 2,500
France and Gt. Britain	New Hebrides	Condominium	5,700	Native Asiatic White	40,000 2,000 1,000

Governing Country	Place	Form of Government	Area (Sq. Miles)	Principal Population Groups (Approx.)	
Gt. Britain	North Borneo	State owned by chartered company	29,500	Native	250,000
				Chinese	50,000
				White	350
				Other	2,000
	Sarawak	Protected State	50,000	Native	350,000
				Chinese	100,000
				White	400
	Brunei	Protected State	2,226	Native	30,000
				Chinese	3,000
				Other	500
	Solomons	Protectorate	11,700	Native	95,000
				White	400
				Chinese	250
	Fiji and Rotuma	Crown Colony	7,083	Native	113,000
				Indian	105,000
				White	4,500
				Chinese	2,200
	Gilbert and Ellice Is., Ocean, etc.	Crown Colony	200	Native	36,000
				Chinese	800
				White	250
	Tonga	Protected Kingdom	250	Native	34,000
				Part-native	450
				White	400
	Pitcairn	Possession	2	Part-native	220
Japan	Marianas	Mandated Territory	245	Native	4,500
				Japanese	45,000
	Palaus		185	Native	6,500
				Japanese	20,000
	Carolines		370	Native	30,500
				Japanese	11,000
	Marshalls		76	Native	10,000
				Japanese	600
	Bonins	Part of Japan Proper	40	Japanese	7,000

Governing Country	Place	Form of Government	Area (Sq. Miles)	Principal Population Groups (Approx.)	
Netherlands	Java		51,030	Indonesian	51,000,000
				Chinese	600,000
				European	220,000
				Other Asiatic	25,000
	Sumatra		182,870	Indonesian	8,500,000
				Chinese	500,000
				European	30,000
				Other Asiatic	35,000
	Dutch Borneo	Netherlands Indies, part of Kingdom of the Netherlands	208,290	Indonesian	2,400,000
				Chinese	170,000
				European	6,500
				Other Asiatic	15,000
	Celebes		72,986	Indonesian	4,750,000
				Chinese	50,000
				European	9,000
				Other Asiatic	15,000
	Lesser Sundas		28,422	Indonesian	4,000,000
				Chinese	20,000
				Europeans	1,750
				Other Asiatic	6,000
	Moluccas		32,422	Indonesian	600,000
				Chinese	6,500
				European	4,500
				Other Asiatic	4,000
	Dutch New Guinea		160,690	Native	450,000
				Chinese	1,500
				European	400
New Zealand	Western Samoa	Mandated Territory	1,130	Native	61,000
				Part-native	3,000
				White	300
				Chinese	300
	Cook Is. and Niue	Dependency	299	Native	17,500
				White	300
	Tokelau Is.	Dependency	7	Native	1,200

136

Governing Country	Place	Form of Government	Area (Sq. Miles)	Principal Population Groups (Approx.)	
Portugal	Port. Timor	Province	7,330	Native	475,000
				Chinese	500
				White	200
United States	Philippines	Commonwealth, in transition to independence	114,400	Filipino	17,000,000
				Chinese	120,000
				Japanese	30,000
				White	19,000
	Hawaii	Organized Territory	6,435	Asiatic	250,000
				White	110,000
				Part-Hawaiian	45,000
				Hawaiian	21,000
				Other	9,000
	Guam	Territory	210	Chamorro	24,000
				White	800
				Filipino	600
				Other Asiatic	800
	American Samoa	Territory	76	Native	13,000
				Part-native	1,500
				White	400

APPENDIX B

A Brief Chronology

Perhaps 500,000 years ago: The Java "ape-man," *Pithecanthropus,* in Java.

Perhaps 25,000 years ago: Australoid and Negritoid type peoples migrate into Malaysia, to be followed from perhaps 8,000 years ago by Indonesian and later by Malayan type peoples.

Probably 500–200 B.C.: First Indian traders and settlers into Malaysia.

Early Christian era: Arabs and Chinese into Malaysia; ancestors of the Polynesians strike out from eastern Malaysia into the South Seas.

413   Chinese pilgrim Fa-Hsien reports on a well-organized state in west Java.

683   Inscription tells of rise of the state of Sri-Vishaya in the Palembang region of Sumatra.

750–850   Building of Borobudhur shrine in central Java.

939   Annam wins its independence from China; nearby states such as Cambodia and Champa are by this time well established.

982   First mention of the Philippines in Chinese records.

1225   Description by Chinese customs official, Chau-Ju-Kua, of the empire of Sri-Vishaya, then at its height.

1292   Marco Polo voyages through Malaysia en route home from China; state of Madjapahit founded in east Java.

1350   Approximate date, estimated from genealogies, for the main Polynesian settlement of New Zealand; Polynesians had spread widely over the eastern islands by this time.

1377   Sri-Vishayan state devastated by Javanese from Madjapahit, then approaching the height of its power.

1405   Grand naval expedition from China, led by Cheng Ho, tours Malaysia, strengthening China's political and commercial influence; further expeditions in 1408 and 1412.

APPENDIX B

1410	Commercial port of Malacca comes under Mohammedan control, and becomes a base for conversion of Malaysia.
1478	Traditional date of conquest of Madjapahit by Moslem forces.
1511–14	Portuguese conquer Malacca and the "Spice Islands" (in Moluccas).
1565	Spaniards establish themselves in the Philippines and western Micronesia.
1596	Dutch expedition to the Indies; by 1641 they had broken Portuguese control in the area.
1768–79	Cook's voyages, charting many of the Pacific Islands.
1788	First British settlements in Australia.
1828	Dutch take control of western New Guinea.
1842	French take over Tahiti and extend control over nearby islands; also annex New Caledonia in 1853.
1863	Plantation development starts in the South Seas, also the "labor traffic."
1874	British annex Fiji; a year later the British High Commission of the Western Pacific is formed to establish law and order in the area.
1881	British North Borneo Co. given a charter to develop North Borneo.
1884	Germans annex northeast New Guinea, British move into Papua; Germany takes the Marshalls a year later.
1887	United States acquires Pearl Harbor in Hawaii.
1898	Spanish-American War; United States takes over Philippines, Guam, and Hawaii.
1899	Samoa is divided between the United States and Germany; Kingdom of Tonga comes under British protection.
1900	Australia's six colonies federated into a Commonwealth.
1906	Britain and France establish a joint "Condominium" in the New Hebrides.
1914	German colonies occupied by the Allies; become League of Nations Mandates in 1920.
1936	Provisional independence given to the Philippines, to become complete in 1946.
1936	United States and Britain establish joint control over Canton and Enderbury Islands.
1939	British, Dutch, and French territories in the Pacific go onto a war footing.

Index

Agriculture, 13, 20, 56, 59–61, 77, 81, 120, 123, Plate 13
Amusements, 116–18; *see also* Dancing, Festivals, etc.
Ancestor cult, 103, 124
Arabia, influences from, 25, 26, 79, 127, 137; settlers from, 25, 29, 56, 72; *see also* Mohammedanism
Arabic language, 32, 38
Architecture, 26, 91–92, 95; *see also* Houses
Art, 16, 26, 50, 78–80, 95, 97, 108, 118–20, 128; *see also* Crafts, Dancing, Music, etc.
Atolls, 13, 54, 62, 66
Austral Islands, 10, 134; *see also* Polynesia
Australia, 39, 138; Aborigines of, 10, 18, 24, 31
Australoid racial type, 10, 18, 19, 23, 24, 137

Bali, 27, 123, 128, Plates 26, 28; *see also* Netherlands Indies, Malaysia
Barkcloth, 79, 94, 106
Birth customs, 110, 118, 123
Borneo, 21, 135; economics, 65, 69, 138; houses, 90–91; people, 22, 135; religion, 123, 126; *see also* Malaysia
Brahmanism, 25, 26, 27, 128
Buddhism, 25, 26, 27, 128
Burial customs, 46, 89, 92–93, 110, 124, 129
Burma, 21, 26, 61, 128

Canoes, 10, 11, 65, 99–101, 123
Caroline Islands, 13, 135; government, 16; language, 35; people, 14, 135; religion, 122; *see also* Micronesia
Carriers, native, 81, 101–02
Celebes, 21, 135; economics, 65; people, 10, 25, 135; religion, 123, 126; *see also* Netherlands Indies, Malaysia
Ceremonies, native, 74, 76, 82, 90, 97, 99, 108, 110–15, 118, 120, 123
Chamorro, 15, 35; *see also* Micronesia
Chiefs, *see* Leaders
Children, 49, 97, 109; games of, 117, 118; the rearing of, 44, 104, 105–06, 110
China, influences from, 21, 25, 27, 32, 34, 98; settlers from, 25, 29, 54, 57, 66, 72, 83, 137
Christianity, influences of, 3, 12, 13, 16, 17, 28, 46, 96, 97, 110, 113, 118, 131; *see also* Missions
Clan system, 44, 82, 85, 106, 113, 120; defined, 108–09
Classes and castes, 71, 107, 113–14
Clothing, native, 3, 20, 43, 51, 94–98, Plates 20, 21
Community, native, 44–45, 85–90, 103–04, 113, 118
Cook Islands, 9, 135; *see also* Polynesia
Cooking, 77–78, 92, 93, 111, Plate 18
Cooperative organization, 58, 67, 68, 72, 81, 84–86, 88, 107
Councils, native, 42, 44–45, 48
Crafts, 16, 50, 56, 69, 73, 78–80, 86, 94, 95, 99; *see also* Arts, Metal working, Tools, etc.
Cults, native, 51, 130–31

Dancing, 12, 13, 92, 112, 116, 117, 118, 119, Plates 23–26
Death, 20, 103, 109, 118, 123, 129
Depopulation, 9, 15, 18
Diet, 54–55, 57, 68, 74–76; *see also* Foods
Dutch, *see* Netherlands

Easter Island, 10, 124–25, 134; *see also* Polynesia
Economics, native, 4, 50, 54–87; and nationalism, 50; and religion, 57–58; and social systems, 59; *see also* Agriculture, Labor, Property, etc.
Education, influence of, 12, 40, 49, 51, 52, 86, 114, 129; native type of, 110; *see also* Schools
Ellice Islands, 9, 42, 73, 134; *see also* Polynesia
Etiquette, 2, 36, 77, 90, 91, 93, 115–16

Family customs, 104, 105–09, 112, 113; *see also* Kinship, Marriage, etc.

141

INDEX

Feasting, 13, 59, 74, 75, 83, 106, 110, 119
Festivals, 82, 90, 97, 118–19, 120; and religion, 124, 127, 128, 129
Fiji, 17, 18, 21, 76, 80, 91, 117, 134, 138; government, 40, 42, 44, 49, 138; language, 31; people, 10, 17, 19, 134, Plate 5; religion, 21, 122, 129; *see also* Melanesia
Fire-making, 77–78
Fishing, 12, 13, 20, 78, 117, Plates 1, 14; place in economic life, 55, 56, 59, 62, 64, 65, 81; poisons, 63; and religion, 58–59, 120, 123
Flores, 19, 123; *see also* Netherlands Indies, Malaysia
Food, native, 16, 54, 55–57, 59–64, 68; consumption habits, 74–77, 86, 110, 116; emergency, 43; preparation of, 77–78, 92, 93, 98, 111; religion and, 75–76, 123, 128; surpluses, 64; taboos on, 62, 128
Forest products, 20, 24, 65, 69, 70
Formosa, 15, 21
French, 39, 138; language influences, 34, 37

German, influence in Pacific islands, 5, 16, 34, 35, 39, 138; missions, 130
Gifts, exchange of, 11, 59, 66–67, 82, 115–16
Gilbert Islands, 134; economics, 60, 67, 73, 83; government, 16, 42, 134; people, 14, 15; religion, 122; *see also* Micronesia
Government, influence of, 3, 21, 27–28, 30, 39–53, 83, 89, 101–02, 109, 130, 137–38; native, 13, 25–27, 39–40; *see also* Law, Rulers, etc.
Great Britain, 39, 40, 134; *see also* specific British territories
Guam, 14, 15, 16, 35, 42, 121, 136, 138; *see also* Micronesia

Hawaii, 9, 11, 12, 30, 73, 136, 138; *see also* Polynesia
Health, 9, 62, 73, 75, 97, 125, 130; native workers, 4, 12, 41, 75; *see also* Medical work
Holidays, 97, 124; *see also* Festivals
Houses, native, 20, 61, 89–94, 105, 120, Plates 20, 23
Household, 45, 58, 67, 84, 91, 92, 104; *see also* Family
Hunting, native, 20, 23, 55, 60, 62, 117

India, influences from, 24, 25–26, 27, 32, 79, 98, 113, 137; Settlers from, 29, 57, 66, 72, 82
Indochina, economics, 64, 83; government, 49, 50, 137; history, 25, 26, 28, 137; people, 21; religion, 128
Indonesian, people, 8, 24–25; political identity, 40; racial type, 19, 23, 24
Inheritance, 47, 86, 105, 128

Japanese, influence of, 4–5, 15, 21, 34, 39, 50, 68, 97; mandated islands, 16, 35, 135; *see also* Carolines, Marianas, etc.
Java, 21, 23, 135; "ape man," 23, 137; arts, 119, 120; economics, 22, 55, 56, 72, 74, 83, Plate 17; houses, 91; history, 25, 26, 27, 137, Plate 7; literacy, 38; nationalism in, 49, 50, 52; people, 23, 28, 29, 33, 73; religion, 123, 125, 128; *see also* Netherlands Indies, Malaysia
Judiciary, native, 45, 46, 47, 48; *see also* Law

Kinship, 13, 58, 59, 65, 68, 84, 88, 104–09, 128; *see also* Family, Clan

Labor, native, 3, 54, 56–57, 68, 69, 80–83; contract, 6, 18, 21, 57, 69, 83; organization, 50; "labor traffic," 5, 138; *see also* Work
Land holding, 4, 47, 110; *see also* Property
Landlords, 56, 68, 71–72, 73
Languages, native, 12, 15, 18, 20, 30–38; common, 31, 33–34, 37, 43; missions and, 30, 34, 37
Law, native, 43–48, 84–85; Islamic influences on, 28, 105, 127–28; religion and, 123
Leaders, native, 8, 12, 28, 39, 44–48, 59, 86, 90, 110; economic position, 59, 76, 84, 85; houses of, 91, 92; nationalism and, 49, 50, 51–52; powers curbed, 46; religion and, 125, 127, 129; social status of, 96, 97, 105, 106, 107, 113–15; women as, 111; *see also* Officials, Rulers
Lesser Sundas, 21, 25, 62, 126, 135; *see also* Netherlands Indies, Malaysia
Literacy, 12, 30, 37–38, 43, 129
Livestock, 54, 60, 64, 92, 102

Malacca, 27, 28, 33, 88, 138

INDEX

Malay Peninsula, 19, 21, 24, 33, 34, 125
Malaysia, economic life, 56, 59, 60, 62, 64, 66, 67, 69, 70, 71, 72, 74, 83, 98, 100; history, 23–28, 137; language, 31; people, 8, 10, 22–29, 137; religion, 122, 127; social customs, 89, 96, 105, 113, 117, 120; *see also* by islands
Maori, *see* New Zealand
Mariana Islands, 13, 14, 16, 35, 135; *see also* Micronesia
Marine products, 20, 55, 56, 57–59, 65, 69, 70; *see also* Fishing
Marquesas Islands, 10, 105, 134; *see also* Polynesia
Marriage customs, 46, 47, 53, 104–07, 109, 113, 118
Marshall Islands, 14, 15, 16, 133, 135, 138; *see also* Micronesia
Medical work, 50, 68; native methods of, 63, 121, 123, 125
Melanesia, economic life, 61, 76, 77, 83, 98; history, 17, 51, 52; language, 20–31; people, 8, 10, 14, 17–21; religion, 116, 122, 129; social customs, 89, 105, 106, 110, 111, 119; *see also* by islands
Metal working, 26, 65, 67, 79, 98
Micronesia, description, 8, 13; history, 138; language, 31, 35; people, 11, 13–16; religion, 121, 129; social customs, 91, 113; *see also* by islands
Migrations, racial, 9–11, 18–19, 23–25, 137; modern, 72–74
Missions, 121–23, 125, 129–30, Plate 30; and language, 30, 34, 37; and social customs, 96, 97, 109, 118; *see also* Christianity
Mixed bloods, 6, 9, 15, 18, 35, 40, 49
Mohammedanism, 125–28; influence of, 3, 27–28, 38, 49, 62, 79, 95, 96, 97, 105, 114, 123, 138
Moluccas, 17, 135; economics, 59, 66; history, 3, 28, 88, 138; language, 31; people, 19, 25; religion, 123, 126, 129; *see also* Netherlands Indies, Malaysia
Money, in native life, 54, 65–63, 69, 70–71, 86, 114; "shell money," 57, 66, Plate 14; "stone money," Plate 15; tobacco as, 77, 83
Music, 12, 78, 82, 118, 119, Plate 26

Nationalism, native, 5, 49–52, 96, 115
Nauru, 14, 16, 134; *see also* Micronesia

Negrito, 18–19, 24, 29, 60, 78, 89; Negritoid type, 19, 23, 137
Netherlands, influence of, 28, 37, 39, 40, 138; Indies government, 39, 42, 73, 135; nationalism, 49, 51, 52; religion, 122; *see also* Malaysia, Java, Sumatra, etc.
New Caledonia, 17, 18, 19, 21, 91, 122, 135, 138, Plate 8; *see also* Melanesia
New Guinea, degree of development, 3, 17, 21, 42; economic, 56, 57, 60, 63, 64, 65, 70, 83; government, 42, 134; language, 31, 34; Netherlands part of, 17, 135, 138; people, 17, 18–19, 20, 24; religion, 122, 126, 130, 131; social customs, 89, 91, 94, 96, 117; *see also* Melanesia, Papua
New Hebrides, 17, 94, 134; economic, 83; government, 42, 134, 138; language, 34; people, 3, 17, 18; religion, 21, 122; *see also* Melanesia
New Zealand, 39, 135; Maori, 9, 11, 12, 30, 79, 137; *see also* Polynesia

Ocean Island, 14, 16, 134; *see also* Gilberts, Micronesia
Officials, native, 3–4, 40, 41, 43–45, 56, 64, 90, 92, 115 *see also* Leaders

Palau Islands, 13, 14, 16, 35, 135; *see also* Micronesia
Papua, 17, 97, 100, 102, 117, 134; government, 42, 138; language, 31, 33, 34; people, 17, 18–19, 24; religion, 130, 131; *see also* Melanesia, New Guinea
Philippines, 21, 136; economics, 60, 62, 67, 71, 73, 83 government, 28, 40, 41, 43; history, 137, 138; language, 34, 38; nationalism, 49–53; people, 10, 15, 19, 22–24, 25; religion, 27, 28, 122, 126, 129, 131; social customs, 94, 96, 111, 113, 117, 120; *see also* Malaysia
Pidgin languages, 33–34, 37
Police, native, 4, 43, Plates 2, 12
Political, *see* Government, Leaders, etc.
Polynesia, 8; economics, 61; language, 30; people, 9–13, 137, Plate 4; religion, 121, 122; social customs, 76, 91, 92, 108, 114; *see also* by islands
Population, 9–10, 13–14, 17–20, 21–23, 103–04, 107, 109; economic aspects of, 56, 61, 71; pressure, 72–74; *see also* Depopulation

INDEX

Ports, influence of, 18, 30, 32, 33, 52, 98; natives at, 13, 69, 73, 86, 92, 126; *see also* Towns
Portuguese, influence of, 21, 28, 32, 33, 34, 39, 136, 138
Property customs, 46, 59, 84–85, 86, 106–07, 110, 113

Race mixture, 6, 9, 15, 18, 23, 24–25; *see also* Mixed Bloods
Racial classification, 9–10, 15, 18–20, 21, 23–25, 137, Plates 4–6
Religion, 3, 12, 16, 21, 25–28, 121–31, Plates 27–30; and art, 118–20, 128; and economics, 58–59, 75, 79, 82–83, 99; holidays, 97; and law, 45, 46; leadership in, 86, 125; and nationalism, 49, 51; new sects, 130–31; old native, 3, 16, 20, 27, 46, 48, 118, 124; rituals, 110–11, 116; sacred places, 11, 89, 91–93, 98, 124; and social customs, 45, 89, 95, 96, 103, 106, 108–11; *see also* Christianity, Mohammedanism, etc.
Rice, cultivation of, 22, 56, 57, 59, 60, 64, 69, 71, 72; diet, 75
Rulers, native, 25, 27, 39, 40, 45, 48, 56, 59, 105, 113–14, 126, Plate 11; *see also* Classes and castes, Leaders

Sacrifices, 46, 92, 124
Sago, 20, 60, 64, 70, 75
Samoa, 7, 135; government, 42, 44, 49, 135, 138; language, 30; people, 9, 11; religion, 129; social customs, 76, Plate 12; *see also* Polynesia
Schools, influence of, 3, 12, 21, 41, 90, 109; and language, 30, 34, 35, 37; missions and, 129; native teachers, 12, 56; *see also* Education.
Self-government, native, 12, 16, 27, 42–45, 47, 50, 52–53
Settlers, white, 28, 41, 54, 67, 84, 88
Settlements, native, 20, 88–90, 103–04; *see also* Community
Sex, 13, 111–12, 116
Social system, 13, 103–20, 129; economic aspects of, 59, 81, 82, 84, 85; status within, 93, 94–96, 97; *see also* Classes, Family, Leaders, etc.
Society Islands, 9, 11, 134, 138, Plate 15; *see also* Polynesia
Solomon Islands, 3, 17, 134; economics, 21, 56, 83; government, 40, 42; language, 33; people, 17, 18, 134; religion, 21, 122; social customs, 79, 94, Plate 20; *see also* Melanesia
Spain, influence of, 15, 16, 27, 28, 32, 33, 34, 35, 39, 49, 113, 129, 138
Spices, 69, 74; trade in, 26, 28, 66
States, native, 25–28, 39–40, 48
Sumatra, 21, 24, 135; economics, 25, 26, 69, Plate 9; history, 25, 26, 137; people, 22, 73; religion, 27, 123, 125–26, 127, 128; social customs, 90, 106; *see also* Netherlands Indies, Malaysia

Taboos, 2, 46, 83, 90, 92; fishing, 58–59; food, 62, 99, 128; house, 90, 92; *see also* Religion
Tattooing, 92, 97
Taxes, native, 3, 6, 68, 69
Thailand, 21, 26, 61, 128
Timor, 3, 17, 19, 28, 59, 123, 135; *see also* Malaysia
Tokelau Islands, 10, 72, 135; *see also* Polynesia
Tonga, 9, 40, 42, 53, 129, 134, 138, Plate 24; *see also* Polynesia
Tools, 3, 16, 79, 98–99
Totemism, 108–09
Towns, natives in, 37, 41, 49, 52, 73, 75, 88, 92, 96, 109, 117, Plate 19; economic conditions, 54, 56, 67–69, 71, Plate 17; *see also* Ports
Trade, native, 3, 12, 20, 25–27, 28, 54, 65–68, 83, 97; influence on language, 30, 34
Travel, native, 1, 68, 89, 99–102, Plate 22
Tuamotu Islands, 10, 11, 134; *see also* Polynesia

Wallis and Horne Islands, 9, 134; *see also* Polynesia
War, native, 1, 12, 17, 20, 40, 46, 47, 51, 65, 89, 113, 117, 118
Wealth, native, 45, 57, 65; *see also* Property
Women, status of, 44, 45, 56, 95–97; and nationalism, 49; religion and, 91, 127; social customs relating to, 105, 109, 110–12.
Work, native, 56, 68–69, 80–83, 108, 110, 111; habits of, 4, 81–82, 86; and religious festivals, 128